DATE DUE			

New Guardians of the Press

Selected Profiles of
America's Women
Newspaper Editors

New Guardians of the Press

Selected Profiles of America's Women Newspaper Editors

EDITED BY

Judith G. Clabes

R. J. Berg & Company, Publishers
Indianapolis, Indiana 46220

To all young women journalists with a dream—and a vision: our best wishes for a bright and happy future.

CONTENTS

INTRODUCTION

I vividly recall the glib words of the speaker at a convention session of the American Society of Newspaper Editors. "The trouble with our times," he said, "is that the future just isn't what it used to be." He wasn't talking specifically about the newspaper business, and he certainly wasn't talking about something so revolutionary as women occupying the editor's office, but what he said may never have been so applicable.

There was a time when the only women who became editors were those who conveniently inherited a newspaper of their very own from extremely generous (and related) benefactors. But the signs of changing times—and "a future that isn't what it used to be"—are everywhere in the newsrooms of our nation's newspapers.

For women, it was only a matter of time. Let them out of the kitchen and they're sure to want to work in the women's section. Let them out of the women's section and they've got crazy ideas about working on the metro desk. It was inevitable that more and more would find their way to the editor's office. And stay.

Still today, at the beginning of the eighties, there aren't many women with their names on the editor's door. But the number is growing. We are more likely to see women in charge at smaller newspapers than at metropolitan dailies. But it's a beginning.

Dorothy Jurney, a retired newspaperwoman who worked for several Knight-Ridder newspapers, does an annual statistical survey of *Editor & Publisher* for the *Bulletin* of the American Society of Newspaper Editors. She takes account of women holding "directing editorships" on the country's daily newspapers. In 1980, Ms. Jurney's survey showed women held a 7.6 percent share of the field—251 positions out of 3,285; only nineteen on papers over 250,000. Among others, the positions considered included editors, executive editors, associate editors, managing editors, deputy and assistant managing editors, and editorial chiefs. In 1982, of 3,281 policymaking positions listed in the *E&P Yearbook,* Ms. Jurney found only 315 were women—9.6 percent. That represented the largest gain in five years. And, she found evidence of more women in "pipeline positions" (jobs leading to top management).

In sheer numbers, women are becoming a force that must be reckoned with. Female college students outnumber males. Females outnumber males, period. Female journalism students outnumber males. It makes sense that practice will catch up with reality. What makes more sense is that practical publishers, eyeing the market, will pay heed to their readers—and there are lots of women readers out there. Research shows, further, that working women—and there are more and more of us—are regular, dependable newspaper readers.

If newspapers are to reflect their communities, and they should, then they must have the right mix across the board. That includes minorities as well as women—in management and on staff. In human terms, that's fair. In management terms, it's smart. It simply makes no sense to overlook a valuable resource out of hand. Promoting the best qualified people is fair.

Yet the old stereotypes that stand in the way of fairness are alive and well. Women are too emotional, the old line goes. Men won't work for them. Women cry when things get tough. Women don't have a head for finances. Women can't take charge.

Well, the old stereotypes don't wash anymore.

No one advocates promotions on the basis of sex, merely the recognition of capable women on the same terms as capable men. One sex does not have all the brains and all the management ability. The truth is that men are more likely to have been given the chance to prove their abilities, and the failure of one man does not end a grand experiment.

There is no gender-linked reason to separate the sexes as to management ability. There is no single style or type of leadership that is preferable or prevalent. All potential leaders need the opportunity to prove themselves, the connections to give them a helping hand and, then, the ability to motivate people. Only culture, society and tradition stand in the way of more women in management ranks. But things change. And the future isn't what it used to be.

At small- and mid-sized newspapers across the country, there are more women in charge than ever before. The numbers are not staggering or astonishing or even equitable, but the barriers have been broken, one at a time.

In choosing the women to share their stories here, I considered the roster of the American Society of Newspaper Editors and the pages of *Editor & Publisher Yearbook*.

ASNE's membership is limited to "directing editors." I limited my search even further. I looked for "editor" and "executive editor" titles and for "managing editor" titles on exceptionally large newspapers. Ultimately, my list was not a large one. It did include all three women presently on the ASNE board of directors and what I considered to be a good mix in regard to circulation and staff size. A few women who met the criteria declined to participate for reasons of their own.

What I got in the end were women willing to share a part of themselves with others, who care about the state of the art and the status of the artists. Together, we hope to be living proof that there is no formula for success, no pattern, no mold that any woman must fit in order to be fit for the top job. We are as different as members of any group could be: ages, backgrounds, experiences—a real diversification.

We seem to be driven, as a group, by a desire to succeed. But the prices we are willing to pay for that success and the compromises we are willing to make are as different as the stories we have to tell. There is the irreverent humor and keen insight of Bev Kees, the sheer gutsiness and determination of Marj Paxson, the thoughtful introspection and resolve of Susan Miller. There is Judy Brown's sense of history and tradition. And Kay Fanning's search for a new life and new adventure in the "last frontier." There is Nancy Woodhull's enthusiasm for risk-taking and Donna Hagemann's early aspirations for the top job. Ann Faragher entered the newsroom through a different door. And Christy Bulkeley's determined to open a lot of doors herself. Mostly, there is the feeling that all of us hope to open the doors for others, too.

Each of us hopes to have something to offer. Certainly, I am grateful to know most of these women personally and glad that you now have the chance to know them, too, and to reap the benefits of their advice, experience and counsel.

I am grateful, most of all, to these women for their caring and for their willingness to share so much of themselves with others.

Happy reading.

Judy Clabes
March 1983

JENNIFER J. ALLEN

JENNIFER ALLEN with managing editor Ray Mayo.

JENNIFER ALLEN with managing editor Ray Mayo.

Jennifer J. Allen

JENNIFER J. ALLEN is editor of the *Daily Sun,* an 11,000 circulation daily and Sunday newspaper serving Corsicana, Texas, and the surrounding seven counties. She is a 1972 cum laude graduate of Ball State University in Muncie, Indiana, with majors in journalism and Spanish and is currently a master's degree candidate in journalism at East Texas State University in Commerce, Texas.

Ms. Allen started her newspaper career as a reporter for the *Brookville, Indiana, Democrat* before joining the *Anderson,* Indiana, *Herald* as assistant lifestyle editor. In 1973, she became wire news and local news editor for the *Journal-News* in Hamilton, Ohio.

She is a member of the Society of Professional Journalists, Women in Communications, Kappa Tau Alpha, the National Association of Press Women, the Texas Association of Press Women, the American Society of Newspaper Editors, Associated Press Managing Editors, and the Association of Business Women of America.

She is active in Corsicana community affairs, serving on the boards of the Red Cross chapter, the community playhouse, and the chamber of commerce.

Ms. Allen has received numerous writing awards.

Failure has never been a word in my vocabulary. For as long as I can remember, I have been expected to strive for more—more knowledge, more skills, more success. Very early in life, my parents made it clear excuses simply were not acceptable: I needed to give 110 percent if I wanted any endeavor to succeed.

Although that disciplined approach was tempered with a large measure of love, those early teachings have made me strive to achieve—from maintaining a 4.0 grade average through school to being named editor of a newspaper.

My formative years, too, are responsible for my love affair with journalism. My home was always filled with books, newspapers, magazines—words of every dimension.

The power of language, both written and spoken, can move mountains and people. Language's power over me has been immense, and my decision to enter journalism was partly an attempt to harness some of that power and to employ it constructively.

1

However, a love and respect for language alone was not sufficient to take me to where I am today.

More than anything else, positive role models made me realize the sky is the limit. These people included my mother, widowed at a young age, who was forced to enter the labor force when the only available jobs for women were secretarial positions, nursing and domestic chores. From her, I learned the value of independence, of being secure with my own identity, of taking a bad situation and turning it to my advantage. I also saw the necessity for being self-sufficient economically, of not depending on others to provide for my needs.

My mother always had a greater vision. She was an "enlightened" woman long before it was fashionable to believe in equality. Therefore, it was natural for me to pick a career that suited my talents rather than a career that would fit around marriage and children. To this day, my mother remains my most trusted friend, adviser and model.

Other helpers along the way included a stern, demanding set of teachers, whose watchwords were, "Yes, you can." I was always encouraged to question, to probe and to challenge.

Those women and men were not concerned about my sex. They were concerned with me. Even after attending college, that background made it impossible for me to believe discrimination existed. To me, it was only a word.

Perhaps fortunately, the real world came knocking when I graduated from Ball State University in Muncie, Indiana, with my prized honors degree in journalism.

On sending out resumes, I found there were only a few beats considered suitable for women. My interests were in police and court reporting; however, editors would only discuss feature reporting with me.

Despite the fact that the women's movement had surfaced a few years earlier, 1972 was not a vintage year for women entering the journalistic field. Most were hired in public relations jobs or for teaching positions. Those of us who were determined to put our futures in newspapers were relegated to soft news.

Thus, I entered the newspaper field as coordinator of teen (high school) correspondents for a mid-sized Indiana newspaper, as well as being a part-time feature writer. Unwittingly, though, that newspaper did me a favor. Through working with those high school students, I gained my first taste of newspaper management and the skills necessary to motivate people and to produce results.

Even though a year later I moved to another newspaper as education beat reporter, I was already aware that at that time women were not equal partners in the reporting world. I became determined not to fall into the same trap.

In 1974, I moved to the copy desk of a mid-sized afternoon daily in southern Ohio, where my real training began. Suddenly, I had to motivate people to write clean copy, make sure everyone met deadlines, and put everything together graphically with sufficient time to meet the daily press start.

Those were heady days, days of real team spirit. It was a time spent working on a newspaper's front lines when I could look at the day's edition and proudly say, "I did that."

Despite the satisfaction with my news editing job, I still wanted more challenges. I yearned to learn more about the greater picture.

As with every person in every newsroom in the United States, I thought I could invent a better mousetrap. I still think that, but I also know enough about the system to realize I was too idealistic in those days.

Luckily, my growing frustration with the routine of my desk job was quickly alleviated. My newspaper—the *Journal-News* in Hamilton, Ohio, which is part of Harte-Hanks Communications, Inc.—tailored a management training program to help me with the skills college journalism didn't provide.

Those college classes helped me learn how to construct a good lead, how to design a pleasing-looking front page, and how to do the mechanical parts of newspapering; however, those classes didn't teach me how to deal with computer printouts, annual budgeting, changing technology, personnel problems, and a myriad of other challenges that are the daily fare of a newspaper editor.

Thanks to that training, in 1979 I was transferred to a Harte-Hanks newspaper in Corsicana, Texas, a town of about 25,000 people. After serving as managing editor there for six months, I was named the *Sun's* editor.

As a woman in an executive position moving from the North to the South I was somewhat of a novelty for Corsicana. However, after the honeymoon ended, my real work began.

I learned quickly that the town wanted more from the editor of its newspaper; it wanted a visible, public figure, someone who could support the town as it grew from an agricultural area to an industrial area, someone who could point out the good as well as the bad.

So, I became active in community life. I realize most journalism students are schooled in what I call creative isolationism. However, after being an editor now for almost three years, I think that theory can be taken too far.

I am on the board of the local chamber of commerce, but I don't feel that compromises my abilities to be an effective journalist. In fact, I think it enhances them.

Through my community endeavors, I am creating more visibility for the newspaper and making my community a better place to live. If that is wrong, then I plan to go on being wrong.

People who once saw the newspaper as something lofty and afar now know it is staffed by living beings, people who are a part of the community they serve.

But don't think it has all been easy. I get my share of "honeys" and "darlings" when I talk to people. I am still asked if the editor is in when I answer my phone.

I also am sure many people think I can be intimidated more easily because I am a woman.

However, people and society do not change overnight. We can legislate equality, but we can't make people operate under its principles until they are ready.

That is what I think separates successful women from nonsuccessful women.

Too many believe an aggressive spirit and talent alone will take them to the top. They won't.

The thing that separates the winners from the losers is an ability to understand people and know what makes each community and each newspaper different. Without that skill, a talented woman will find herself passed over again and again for a promotion.

Success also takes tact—knowing when to press ahead and knowing when to go along with the system. Compromise and teamwork need to be lifetime mottos.

It also means swallowing your pride and ignoring the times you are called "honey." It means forgetting your feminine wiles and blending into the management group. Batting your eyes might be fun after work, but don't do it at the office.

If you want people to take you seriously, then you have to take yourself seriously. And that means talking, thinking, interacting, dressing and behaving sensibly at all times.

This isn't to say a female executive shouldn't have a sense of humor. She should, but she also needs to avoid being brash, abrasive, pushy and obnoxious. While our male counterparts may be able to get away with such actions, a woman with all those qualities is quickly labeled a bitch.

Then there is the trap of playing sexual politics. This, ladies, must be avoided at all costs. Even though you know you're not sleeping your way to the top, there will always be those who are ready to accuse you of it at the slightest provocation.

Your behavior must be above reproach. You can go out with the boys after work, but don't take that one drink too many. Don't cry at the office when things don't go your way. Drown your pillow with tears if you need to, but do it at home.

And don't drown your co-workers with your problems. Keep your own counsel. My best support system has always been myself. It's not that I have the rare ability to remedy all that ails me professionally and personally; however, how can I expect those who work for me and those in parallel and superior positions to respect me and my judgments if I run wailing to them every time a dark cloud appears on the horizon.

Successful women in journalism have two distinct qualities: (1) an ability to be secure in their own femininity without being overtly sexual, and (2) an ability to think "like men." I realize that is a chauvinistic statement, but I stand by it.

Women who follow in the typical stereotypes of our sex will never succeed, from the meek little girl who never grows up to the loud, domineering soul who angers everyone in sight.

Observe the men around you. Notice how they employ the buddy system. See how they tackle the big problems without wringing their hands. Watch how they normally remain calm during a professional crisis. Of course, there are exceptions to the rule, but we could learn a lot by blending into the system rather than fighting to remodel it to fit our preconceived notions.

I have noted, too, how difficult it is for women to work within the buddy system. Most of us really weren't reared to be team players. Other girls were simply that—other girls, people to compete against for the most handsome date to the prom.

It is the "me versus them" trap, commonly called the queen bee syndrome. In essence, this mentality sees itself as special while all other women are merely drones within the professional hive.

I've felt it myself, so don't think I'm totally innocent. I won't lie; it is a tremendous ego boost to attend professional meetings and be virtually the only woman. Everyone remembers your name; everyone wants to buy you dinner; everyone wants to sit with you. It's wonderful, but it's also a trap.

It is time we broke out of that mold and started to think of our peers as people: some male and some female, all of whom should be judged on their individual merits and personalities, not their sex.

And by the same token, you should judge yourself by your own merits, not by standards from textbooks or by what you think you should be. When you are able to look at yourself and give an honest appraisal of the negative as well as the positive qualities, then you are on the road to success.

That belief colors almost everything I do, from decision making to handling stress.

In a similar vein, I want each employee to continually prove himself or herself. I don't want excuses; I want valid reasons. I want each employee to keep growing, and the only way to ensure that happens is to be a good listener, guide with a steady hand, don't play favorites, mete out even discipline and provide daily challenges.

That, essentially, is my management style. Not that it's always successful; it isn't. I've certainly had my share of disappointments. But it is what works most of the time for me.

Even though my title is editor, I see myself more as a teacher than an administrator. The heart of any good newspaper is a professional reporting and desk staff. Each must be good individually and as a member of the team. And the only way to help maintain that level of quality is to teach and demonstrate those skills.

With my boss, I take the same even-handed approach I do with my employees. If I don't know the answer to a question, I say so, and I attempt not to take criticism as a personal attack but as healthy instruction.

In many ways, I have always been fortunate to have very demanding bosses. Just as I hope my employees see me as someone who can help them achieve new levels, I look at my superior as an individual who can help me in that same way.

As in my dealings with the community, my peers and my staff, I refuse to become embroiled in heated arguments with my boss. Of course, there are times when my boss and I are light-years apart philosophically, but confrontation only heightens the differences.

Although I am hardly a retiring mouse, I also know there are times when it is best not to start a major conflict over something there is no hope of modifying.

I don't advocate being a yes-man (or yes-woman), but always being the dissident voice will only hamper your career track and will foster bitterness.

Criticism has always been the hardest thing for me to accept. However, I think that is what has made me grow the most. My advice to aspiring female journalists would be to learn how to deal with criticism. Learn it early and don't forget how beneficial criticism can be.

React minimally when criticism is given. Don't take it personally. Use what is helpful and discard the rest. And develop a thick skin. A perpetually bruised ego will injure you professionally as well as personally.

Young journalists should not expect the moon without considerable effort. Don't expect to merely do a good job and be promoted. That's just not the way reality is structured.

In addition to doing a good job, be willing to voluntarily—yes, that means without expecting overtime pay—accept new assignments and challenges. That means proving yourself and earning a chance to see how management functions.

Getting ahead also means you must become your own public relations agent. Let your bosses know you are interested in knowing more about the overall picture. Learn all you can about your company or prospective companies. Simply wanting to get ahead isn't enough; it takes drive, time and perseverance.

If you wait to get noticed, though, you might wait a long time. If you have an annual or semiannual evaluation with your superior, use that time to express your desire to learn more and to go further.

But remember this: Success exacts a price, and it isn't cheap.

For me, there are long hours, holidays spent at the office so my employees can spend the day with their families, weekend work compiling special reports and constructing the annual budget. Along the way, there also was a divorce.

I find, too, that I have to resist the temptation to try to be Superwoman. I would like to do it all, but it is difficult when you realize you can't.

Sometimes the loneliness is overwhelming. Are the people I call friends really my friends or merely so because I am editor of their community newspaper? Mainly, the latter. The real friends are rare and should be treasured.

And there is the age-old question of men. My experience is that most men are fascinated by a woman in my position; however, that fascination quickly fades. Soon that turns into a series of one-upmanships, designed to reassure the average man that his ego is intact.

Like those rare, real friends, that rare, real relationship is difficult to find. I think I have built such a relationship with someone, but it has been years in the making. However, he falls among the rare—a man who is not threatened by a successful woman, who does not feel emasculated if tomorrow brings a job offer and we have to move to the city of my choice, who understands my long hours and is supportive.

I wouldn't trade my world for any other, but it hasn't been easy and it won't get easier. Just as I wouldn't recommend journalism for everyone, I wouldn't recommend being an editor to everyone.

In my case, it was the right path. I'd do it all again, even the mistakes.

If effective, an editor leaves a lasting legacy in both the product she develops and in the people who carry her ideals with them throughout their career.

For me, that makes it all worthwhile.

New Britain Herald

JUDITH W. BROWN

New Britain Herald

JUDITH W. BROWN

Judith W. Brown

JUDITH W. BROWN is editor and publisher of the *New Britain,* Connecticut, *Herald,* an afternoon daily with a circulation of almost 42,000. She became editor in 1969 and publisher in 1975.

Since graduation from Mount Holyoke College, she has worked at the *Herald* as a reporter; music, art and drama critic; modern living page editor; editorial writer and executive editor.

Mrs. Brown was the first woman elected to the board of directors of the American Society of Newspaper Editors and is serving a second three-year term. She has served on a variety of ASNE committees. She was also the first woman president of the New England Society of Newspaper Editors and is still a member of its board of governors. She is former president of the Connecticut Daily Newspaper Association and has been a judge and jury chairman for the Pulitzer Award's committee five times.

In 1979, she received the Yankee Quill Award from the New England Academy of Journalists for outstanding achievements in New England. In 1982, she was named Woman of the Year by the New Britain Business and Professional Women's Club.

She is married and is the mother of four children: Amy, 20, a junior at Carnegie-Mellon University; Vance, 19, a sophomore at Brown University; Heather, 17, a freshman at Mount Holyoke College; and Christable, 16, a junior at Loomis-Chaffee School.

She is a board member of the New Britain Museum of American Art, the Burritt Mutual Savings Bank, AAA of Hartford, and the YWCA.

Some people think that I was born and raised an only child. Not so. There was another child in the family. It was the newspaper, and sometimes it got more attention than I did.

As I sit at my terminal and glance at faded pictures of my grandfather, who was one of the founders of the *Herald,* I realize that a newspaper needs the nurturing and interest that someone who cares can give it. Someone has always cared about the *Herald,* and, interestingly, three of these people have been the women of three different generations, all mothers, all coming from the different orientations a period of time can give. The *Herald* is 102 years old and this caring is part of its heritage.

The family involvement with newspapers began when my grandfather, Robert J. Vance, ran a small weekly newspaper called the *Observer,* which dates back to 1876. In 1880, the *Herald* was started by a printing company as a weekly also and it became a daily in 1883. In 1887, my grandfather decided to join the *Herald* as editor, despite having taken several shots at the new publication, including a pointed dissertation about its nameplate which he said looked like an explosion in a tool factory. At that time our home city was the Hardware City of the World, a reality which the *Herald* had tried to incorporate into its nameplate by spreading the implements of the trade far and wide.

Shortly thereafter he went to Congress and married a Washington lady, who considered Connecticut Yankee territory but, nevertheless, came back here with him. In 1902 at age forty-eight, my grandfather died, leaving my grandmother with three children, ages eleven, ten and eight. Since he had died of tuberculosis, she thought it would be a practical idea to take the little family out west. For two years she roamed around the New Mexico of the early 1900s, often pacing the porches of the boarding houses waiting for a check from home. The children were blissfully free of studious pursuits. One day a letter came from the judge of probate, telling her that if she did not get home, she would lose the *Herald* because of an inept business manager. Back she came and took over the reins of the paper. Some of her tenacity and the quality of her guidance are reflected in these quotes from the obituary in her newspaper in June 1938:

"Through the incessant worries of the years when the *Herald* was in its infancy until the time when it arrived at its present estate, an institution in the life of New Britain, Mrs. Vance showed unusual executive ability. Through stormy seas and in calm waters, she constantly remained an inspiration to the working force.

"When dark clouds obscured the horizon, it was the force of her indomitable courage that brought victory. When problems beset the adolescent organization, it was her iron will that overcame almost insurmountable obstacles. Her kindly heart infused all within her ken with a spirit that has brought the *Herald* to the forefront among publications in the state."

While waiting for her sons to return from World War II my grandmother ran the paper from her home and through her daughter, my mother, who worked in the newsroom covering the news, social events and things that women reported in those days. When my older uncle returned he assumed the title of managing editor pretty much running the paper until his death in 1951. In the meantime, my mother had taken time from the paper to bring me up, not returning until 1959 when she became editor and publisher at the age of sixty-seven, really too late to effect too much. Her older brother had died in 1951, the other having served as editor and publisher until 1959.

Although I realize that one cannot live in the past, my publisher's office and memorabilia, plus the general tone, acknowledge that there is a heritage which, in effect, propels me into the present and future. These relics of another time—buttons from the newsboys' dinner of 1897, a zinc plate from our hot metal days, a picture of the *Herald* staff (all men) taken before 1902—remind me constantly of the tradition that I am carrying on.

Having come up on the news side and feeling as I do that the job of editor is the most important in the newspaper, I have always had an office in the news department. Actually it is a very tiny office which was originally planned as the office for a secretary to the adjoining larger room, which now serves as my publisher's domain. The two offices were described as follows in a recent article in the *New Haven Register:* "The publisher's office is a shrine to newspapers in general and the *Herald* in particular. Old prints, posters, a stand of wooden type crowd together in a warm clutter. Some of the big front pages of this century hang beside an enlarged sketch of the young Victorian newsboy used throughout the *Herald's* centennial celebrations last year.

"The room is rich in atmosphere, full of Judy Brown's memories and personality. But it is far from a disorderly, unbusinesslike place. The large Victorian desk in the corner may be covered by papers, but each has its place. And the editor's office through the connecting open door has a much-used video display terminal.

"And the paper is obviously a ruling passion. Brown is not so much aware of being a woman in an unusually powerful position as she is of being the successor to blood relatives who poured their time and passion into the same paper—though she is particulary proud of succeeding her grandmother, 'who held on to the *Herald* for her children when grandfather died,' and of her mother, who took over as editor and publisher when she was already elderly."

It was not always so, of course. When I began as a reporter in 1951 after graduation from Mount Holyoke College, there were two liabilities which I shouldered—the first being that I was of the family, the second that I was a woman. At that time, it was assumed that I would do simple things like calling about society news, and that my boy cousin would in due course become the publisher of the paper. Naturally, I rebelled and the city editor put me on general reporting, which included covering the teacher's college in New Britain and all of the speeches at the all-male luncheon service clubs. There was many a startled look in those male bastions when

I arrived at the old hotel dining room to write up the luncheon talks, which on occasion were salty tales indeed! In those days, there was no such thing as a publicity director at the college and daily I would take the bus and wander around, talking at random to professors and students about what was going on. Sometimes I came up with stories that the president didn't like too well, but I think I found out more from prowling the halls than we do today with the efficient press releases handed out by publicity people.

In those days covering sports was strictly a masculine prerogative. Nevertheless, one day I was sent on an assignment to give the woman's angle on a high school football game. Naturally wanting to be with my "fellows," I climbed, or tried to climb, the stairs to the press booth. The uproar was worse than that going on on the field. I can't imagine to this day what was going on up there, but the event attracted a great deal of publicity including a story which appeared in a downstate paper known as somewhat of a scandal sheet.

Probably the most important story I covered during those early years was the purchase in 1953 of four murals, The Arts of Life in America, from the Whitney Museum by the New Britain Museum of American Art. The artist, Thomas Hart Benton, was due at the museum to touch up the murals, and I was sent to do the interview. Before leaving on the assignment, I visited the library to read up on this famous American artist, so that I would not waste his time and mine asking questions which were readily supplied in books. Then, in the company of the three masculine old pros who covered the art beat for other newspapers, I met the artist, a tiny man, dwarfed by his gigantic murals, with peppery black eyes. The others started the routine questioning, birthplace, etc., wasting much time. Then the museum director brought out a pitcher of martinis, and who was I to affirm that I just couldn't drink with the boys? Drink we did and I, who was going to go home early and start the story, went home and slept until 6 A.M. It was then that I discovered what deadline pressure can be! I had also learned, however, that research pays off so that I had the everyday tools readily at hand and could concentrate on the original quotes and impressions. Lesson to women—do your homework and don't feel it is necessary to drink like a man!

Although it provides the continuity, being a member of the family is no guarantee of success or respect. In fact, it can lessen when you are third generation, for people are likely to regard you as getting more feeble minded as these generations pass like the French kings of the eighteenth century! No matter where you start, and I have had a succession of news-related jobs, do not expect anyone to figure you to have any brains at all, especially if you are a woman. When I became editor in 1969, I wrote an editorial on what it means to be an editor. One of the local factory executives was just leaving the newsroom and stopped by my office. "I really enjoyed your editorial," he said, "but did you really write it?" I don't suppose I would have had the understanding a fellow male would have had if I had hit him!

It is my opinion anyway that people are much more tolerant of an heir apparent than of an heiress apparent. It is all right for the sons of the family to raise a little hell, go hunting in the far north, drink with the boys. But a woman, and this is probably true of any woman in an executive position whether she is a direct descendent of the founder or not, must be extremely cautious and prove herself capable in her job over and over again. There just isn't, nor can there be, the same casual give-and-take as there is among the guys. My uncle, for instance, would go everyday after deadline to the hotel next door with his pals from the news and mechanical departments for some afternoon camaraderie.

In thinking back on it now, I can see, however, that much progress has been made: I was the only woman, for example, in my API class in 1961 for top news executives; now there are many in that capacity. I was the first woman to become president of the New England Society of Newspaper Editors; now there are two on the board. I was either the first woman to be elected to the board of the American Society of Newspaper Editors (or second if Oveta Culp Hobby back in the forties was elected—no one seems to know); now there are three on the board and several committee chairpersons. Also I was the third woman since 1960 to receive the Yankee Quill Award from Sigma Delta Chi, New England Academy of Journalists in 1979. Actually, in the newspaper publishing world, I feel that women are accepted as equals and I have had no difficulties, except with the thought of going to China in the early 1970s as the only woman delegate of ASNE. The then-president called me to say that the chairman of the committee could not go and as vice-chairman I was eligible. "Besides," he added, "I need a dame." I trust he spoke in jest!

Appropriately, two of my daughters were literally born into the newspaper world. While I was expecting my first baby in 1961, the New Britain Press Club (then all men) had scheduled a tour of the hospital. My baby decided to arrive that night, so I was wheeled to the delivery room in full labor while my compatriots straggled down the hall. It was hard to tell who was more unsettled by the encounter. My third daughter and last baby was nearly born as I sat in a small office with the chief editorial writer to whom I was apprenticed at the time. For some reason neither of us had a watch, so as my pains came, he would wheel back and forth into the hall to check the timing. As the pains got closer, he suggested, somewhat palely, that I had better get to the hospital, took me down in the freight elevator, bade me farewell and scampered back up the stairs leaving me to go home, call my husband and get to the hospital somehow.

The responsibilities of the working mother—be she editor or publisher or whatever—are rich and varied. When the children are young, one must learn to be a master weasel on the car pool. It is the time of contagious diseases, so one must have the means of setting up an office at home on a moment's notice because you cannot send a child with chicken pox off to nursery school (although he probably caught it there), nor can you ask someone in to take care of a houseful of children all throwing up at once. There are times then that you are simply going to have to stay home. In order to compensate for this, you can rationalize the days missed as sick days, which means of course you cannot get sick yourself!

It is hard and sometimes very frustrating not to be able to go to the elementary school plays and concerts because they come during the day; it is hard always to have to say no to being a Brownie Scout leader; it is hard to do a great, special job on making a birthday cake look like a carousel; and it is hard to try to give everything and everybody his or her due.

It is absolutely essential that the working mother be organized so that the little everyday things, like not having planned anything particular for supper, do not throw you off into expending energy on things that could have been avoided. You can be sure on the day that four hungry children and a husband are all demanding dinner, you will get a phone call from someone who wants to keep his name out of the paper because this is the first and only time he ever shoplifted; the dog will nip a passing jogger; you will have to take your daughter around to deliver her Girl Scout cookies right this minute; a child will have to have cupcakes for school the next day; and someone will call about a mistake in a headline. It turns into a day like we had at the office when the computer system went down completely and President Carter had planned the abortive rescue attempt in Iran.

It is fairly easy to keep yourself organized and sometimes easy to plan a day at work, but to have everyone else in the family tell you his or her plans is difficult, especially as the children get to be teenagers and never know what they are going to be doing until a minute before.

A working mother has no leisure time whatsoever and this must be recognized as immutable. There is no time to read anything but newspapers, which also fortunately counts as part of the job for an editor; very little time for friends (of course, the editor of a community newspaper usually ends up with everyone in town being angry with her or him sooner or later); no time to give any kind of a party, except for children's birthdays; and certainly no time for the community.

In most communities, the publisher of the newspaper is always invited and expected to serve on bank boards, United Way, symphony boards, community revitalization, chamber of commerce, etc., etc. As editor and publisher of the paper, however, I consider that I serve the community everyday through news coverage and editorials, so am somewhat ambivalent as to whether it is really necessary to serve in person. Nevertheless, if one is a working mother, something has to give and, in my case, it was this that I did not participate in. Certainly the meetings of these organizations take away from time spent with the children. But if one feels that it is necessary to do something within the community, then there are plenty of service jobs in which you can work along with the kids, but STAY OUT OF POLITICS. Certainly no school boards or any jobs which require an election. An editor or publisher should run quickly away from any job that involves politics, even though I recognize that my grandfather was a congressman. Of course, his own newspaper supported him while the others screamed loud and long about the red-headed upstart who required the Democratic party to change its platform before he would accept the nomination. The fact that he won probably proves that it was good to have at least one newspaper, even if it's your own, behind you . . . but those were other times and sincere newspaper editors and publishers of today would not be able to reconcile this with what we stand for.

It might sound from all of this that it has been very easy and that I have had no problems whatsoever, but there are aspects which have been neither easy nor pleasant, and I was not prepared for them by education or by temperament. Although in my adult life I never knew my Uncle Jack, who was managing editor and literally ran the paper for thirty years, I have heard that he loved a good fight. As far as I'm concerned there are very few "good" fights and the one that I have lived with for these many years has not been one of them.

The *Herald,* of course, is a family business and this is both its uniqueness and its liability. It has always demanded the best from the three generations that have guided it and, although they have railed sometimes and threatened, not one of these generations has wanted to sell it. With a family business, one always runs the risk of a fight. Fortunately, my fight was not with blood relatives, but with lawyers and banks who managed to keep up the struggle long after those of the family were gone. They made me pay dearly for what I considered rightfully mine and for the betterment of which I had striven all of my working life.

Stock arrangements are unique to every family and my grandmother had taken care of her own children and the three grandchildren, making sure that her own children benefited until the last was gone and that the two grandchildren of one family were equal to the one in the other family (myself). Most people would have divided it like a pie into three equal parts. My grandmother did not follow what might have been natural to many of us, for when she made her will, we three were children. I was working at the paper as a reporter when my cousin, a sophomore at Yale, died following a pre-Christmas vacation automobile accident. With that tragedy died my uncle's hopes for succession, as my other cousin lived in New York City and abroad and was not interested in staying at home to work at the paper.

My uncle's will tied up the stock that came to my remaining cousin from our grandmother into a trust over which she had no control, giving that to his wife upon his death in 1959. At this time, my mother became editor and publisher, running the paper with my father as her helpmate in the business department. Both were then in their sixties. During this time, I was serving my apprenticeship of five years in the editorial department, writing editorials, editing letters and columns, laying out the page, and doing reviews. I was also busy having babies, four in four and a half years, three girls and a boy. It was a good time. The paper did well financially. I was able to structure my hours so that I could rush home between editorials to nurse the babies, and fortunately, I had housekeepers who were able to help with the everyday chores. My husband taught at a country day school nearby so that he could get home quickly if a problem developed. The usual things happened—caring for three children all sick with chicken pox at once, a trip to the hospital on Christmas night with a child with croup, a nursemaid who told my son that if he didn't get into bed for his afternoon nap a witch would come out of the closet, a three-year-old who cut off her sister's golden curls.

When my mother died in 1975, my corporate world became a tougher place. My aunt returned from Florida demanding to "run" the paper; my father, still grief-stricken, had to cope with evaluations and realign the corporate structure, but my cousin returned from Spain and we reestablished our old friendship. Although we had followed different life styles, she was delighted to find a family to become an aunt to and our common heritage and genuine affection for one another helped to reestablish a bond. She still had no interest in being part of the company and was willing to leave it to me to handle.

During the next year, the *Hartford Times* folded and we decided to expand our coverage and circulation into three other towns. This proved to be a monumental effort, as we first tried to incorporate nine towns into one edition, finally deciding to go to two editions with major replating of several pages. It was a nightmare to begin with, but now it all has been accomplished so smoothly that I can hardly remember the problems we went through. When we started we had 32,000 circulation paid; we are now the third largest afternoon daily in the state, with almost 42,000 circulation.

Viewed in human terms, things became more painful. In the summer of 1976, my aunt died and with her much of the animosity of the corporate struggle. My father who had been a fine support to me throughout all of this died in October 1977, and my cousin, with whom I was now looking forward to sharing the spirit if not the running of the *Herald,* died two weeks later of cancer at the age of forty-eight. It was a black time for me emotionally, and soon the lawyers and the banks moved in to sue, disparage and try to manipulate the company which had been part of my life force. Fortunately, the support system was not all gone and the person who is general manager and president of the company proved to be a lawyer, counselor and friend at a time when all were desperately needed. Subpoenas were served as the bank sought to claim my cousin's stock; depositions served; pressure to sell the whole business put on me; unpleasant implications made.

Throughout it all, the paper had to be kept on course, so most of this had to remain buried inside because these are certainly not the kinds of vibrations one wants to give out. Finally an agreement has been reached and gradually I am buying what I consider should rightfully be mine. The bitterness and hurt remain.

As I look back now on the years, I cannot find any great pearls of wisdom to pass along to women following a similar career. It is important to believe, of course, that all things are possible and to love what you are doing. Thus, the greatest support system comes from within.

Women have found newspaper work particularly compatible in all areas of endeavor, from columnists to publishers. About two years ago, all three winners of the American Society of Newspaper Editors' writing awards were women. As a matter of fact, some of this country's most outstanding columnists are women. Many careers show that it is possible to have a family and run a newspaper as well. It takes a division of time, of course, but you can often supplement one to the enrichment of the other. It helps to have support from the people you work with and at home.

Naturally, if I had been a man I would have done things differently, but I do not believe that I would have gained the recognition of being somewhat unique in a world where women editors and publishers are still not that common.

As a matter of fact, I will go out on a limb and say that being a woman in today's newspaper world can be an advantage. The opportunities are many and the acceptance has been won. Professional organizations such as the American Society of Newspaper Editors and Sigma Delta Chi have proven themselves concerned and interested in encouraging women in editorial and newspaper management positions. ASNE has been actively seeking qualified women members since 1973 when I did a survey on women in journalism.

Just last fall, I was involved in a conference between New England and Soviet editors. There were no women in the Soviet delegation, and they told us that the only women editors in the Soviet Union were with women's magazines. The New England delegation had two women and could report favorably about women in newspapers in this country.

Actually, I think it is probably a good time to be a woman. All careers are open to them, and they are being accepted into more and more professions. It is a time of choice and a time of all kinds of help for getting things done quickly. Sometimes I tremble for the family, but I guess working mothers will always have a bit of a guilt complex, which can be compensated for, at least in the newspaper profession, by making the youngsters more aware of the interesting world of news with which we live. It can be fun, as the children get older, to take them to conventions. I will never forget the jackpot we hit at the Associated Press Managing Editors convention in Disney World, Florida, when my twelve-year-old son and my ten-year-old daughter saw the first Skylab go up; heard President Nixon declaim, "I am not a crook;" danced to a Dixieland band; and my daughter even had her steak cut up by Howard Baker!

This incident helps to illustrate the fact that newspaper editors are where things are happening and where political and governmental leaders appear. For a community newspaper such as ours, however, this is as true and as important on a local level as the nation is to such newspapers as the *New York Times*. As I wrote in the foreword to our centennial edition, published in October 1981, "In its relationship to New Britain, the *Herald* has played a unique and special part, one which is duplicated by nothing else. The newspapers contain a continuous record of the people, places and events that have figured in this city's development throughout the past century. Residents turn to its bound volumes for genealogies, for facts about places that have disappeared, for an understanding of things as they occurred, not as summed up years later; editorials and letters on local subjects comment, not in the wisdom of hindsight, but only within the limited scope of each day. Many articles belong just to New Britain, while others reflect and localize events that were happening in the nation and the rest of the world."

Working on that special commemorative edition, days, nights and weekends, with personal concentration on the history of the *Herald,* I became more and more aware of its heritage and my own. Since no member of the family was around to share that moment when the centennial edition came off the press, I experienced a great letdown; yet during the preparation, I felt very close to those who put so much of their lives and hope into it. My thoughts went back especially to my grandmother who fought hard to keep the paper going for her children, and I, too, felt that if it is possible to hand over to one's children a tradition with the meaning and strength of three generations behind it, then this is indeed something of value. With a newspaper, of course, you are not passing along just a business of three generations but an honored tradition of a free press in a free society, which has behind it the continuity of 300 years. In my own case, having lived with and believed in the newspaper all of my life, I have tried to pass along this feeling for it to my children. I think the newspaper and what it represents are very important; perhaps the next generation will think so, too, someday.

CHRISTY C. BULKELEY

CHRISTY BULKELEY covered the 1972 Democratic Convention in Miami along with (from left) Bill Ringle, Jack Germond and John Quinn.

Christy C. Bulkeley

CHRISTY C. BULKELEY has been editor, publisher and president of the *Commercial-News* in Danville, Illinois, since 1976 and a vice-president of Gannett Central Newspaper Group since 1981. Prior to her Danville position, she was editor, publisher and president of the *Saratogian* in Saratoga Springs, New York, and editorial page editor of the *Times-Union* in Rochester, New York.

A 1964 graduate of the University of Missouri-Columbia, Ms. Bulkeley is a member of the American Society of Newspaper Editors, the American Newspaper Publishers Association, the Associated Press National Nomination Committee, Women In Communications (national president, 1975), Sigma Delta Chi, the Missourian Publishing Association, the Inland Press Association, and the Eastern Illinois University Students Publications Advisory Board.

In Danville, she is a member of the area chamber of commerce board of directors, the YWCA board of directors, the Danville Area Community College Foundation, the Executive Club and the Danville Area Economic Development Corporation board of directors.

She received the Illinois Municipal Human Relations Association Award in 1982 and the WICI Headliner Award in 1978. She delivered the Siebert Lecture at Michigan State University in 1978 and is listed in *Who's Who of American Women*. She was named one of the "Leaders of the Future" in 1976 by the National Council of Women.

She is married to P. David Finks who holds a Ph.D. in sociology.

The Argus girls came to town in the early 1950s, started a weekly which soon was the only weekly in town, then the flagship of their chain of three.

The assistant prosecuting attorney told me shortly before I graduated from college in 1964 that I'd never make it to Washington as a reporter unless I'd sleep with the editor.

I went off to my first job with the former as my model, the latter as an amusing incident tucked away in memories.

Two weeks after starting that first job (as the city desk's editorial assistant), I wrote in my journal:

"In the longer run, not only do I have to convince people I'm as good as I think I can be, but I also have to convince them women can be

23

newspapermen, too. They in reality don't admit this as readily as I'd been led to believe."

The clues had been available, had I chosen to accept them. The parting shot from my last great college crush was (according to the journal):

"Yes, we'll probably run into each other when I'm vice-president of NBC in New York City . . . and you're a society editor out there."

I added: "We laughed . . . by the time he is vice-president of NBC, by gosh, we'll see who knows where to find whom first."

In the fall of 1982, these situations came at me within a few days of each other:

—The Society of Professional Journalists, Sigma Delta Chi, produced a national convention program that was ninety percent male. The society's membership is nearly fifty percent female.

—The Journalism Education Committee of the Associated Press Managing Editors association issued its report on journalism education in 1990, the result of interviews with forty-nine journalists and journalism educators. One or two (a neuter name) were women—the other ninety-six percent (obviously) were men.

—Father Theodore Hesburgh, president of Notre Dame, spent five minutes of luncheon remarks before 150 people at a journalism ethics conference eulogizing Cassie Mackin, whose death from cancer had been reported the day before. As he talked about the tough, smart, persistent, professional model she established for all—NOT just women—I nearly cried.

She was all that Father Ted said. But she was more. She was from my generation, the first generation when bright, talented, ambitious and persistent journalists who happened to be female had a chance at the jobs that would command their abilities. And she was the first to die.

Will the rest of us live to see the day when we aren't curiosities or extraordinary threats or expected to be better to get the same opportunities?

Eighteen years. Nearly thirty, if you count from when I started working for the Argus girls as a high school student. Or twenty-five, if you count from the time the publisher of the daily serving my home offered me a blank check for the long-haul future.

July 28, 1964, while reporting to the journal about the just-ending Rochester, New York, riots, I wrote:

"Sunday I didn't work—what had to be done wasn't what women could do (even I'll admit that), since it was all in the scene of the jail environs."

Not in the journal but still vivid are the city editor's orders that

Saturday:

First, when he called at 6 A.M. (I was the last person called; the riots had started around midnight), he ordered me to park in the nearby underground garage and run to the guarded back door.

Second, when we all quit for the day, he ordered the women (both of us, the third was on vacation) to go straight home, to stay home until we came to work Monday.

And I remember hanging up on an uppity *New York Herald Tribune* editor who "young ladied" me once too often.

July 18, 1965: Work has gotten better ever since I got a raise at the end of the month and moved off the busy work desk. I'm now covering town government in addition to the beats I've had since early this year and also am general assignment whenever they need me. . . .

(1982 note: I went to meetings on my own time at night, wrote the stories at work and followed up mostly by phone as appropriate.)

. . . The town bit is great—I've a pretty free hand in twelve of them. . .

. . . One other thing: I've spent one day in Albany and one in Washington, D.C., both with bureau reporters. The trips assured me that's where I want to go—Albany first, then Washington. . . .

(1982 note: Those visits were at my own expense on days off.)

Now that I've seen how a bureau reporter has to work, the range his work covers and speed and pressure he's under, I know I've much to learn before I'll have a chance to do the kind of job I want to.

And at last I am learning it by covering the assignments I am. I hesitate to set up a timetable—and there aren't any women legislative correspondents in Albany at this point—but the path is clear.

(1982 note: From almost the beginning, I had been going to city council meetings on my own time, determined to learn all I could. Reaction from the beat reporters and politicians was mixed. Soon I was going to the in-control party's post-mortems after council meetings and was able to pass tips and ideas on to our paper's reporter.

(In September 1982, I chanced upon one of the reporters from that year, one who barely acknowledged my presence during the year before he moved on. I was amused to note his claiming credit, as he introduced me to colleagues at the same party, for my progress.)

August 7, 1965: I have a promotion of sorts. Starting Monday, I become the Irondequoit reporter—which means I have a whole town and am responsible for whatever goes on in it—to the tune of about four columns of news a day. . . . I'll be completely on my own and free to develop the beat however I see fit.

February 6, 1966: The city editor has promised me a crack at city hall "maybe not for six months," but it's been decided.

June 30: Something came up that demanded both political-government reporters full time, so this week I kind of took over the county government. . . . Tuesday night I had the city council meeting—a pretty big meeting—by myself and was to have had a supervisors meeting (working overtime). But a special city council meeting was called for this morning so I covered it and some other people did supervisors.

This afternoon Herb said I'll be covering city hall while the regular goes on politics for the duration of the campaign at least, and county government too.

This was the long-run plan as I'd understood it, but not to go on this soon. The story that gave me my break hastened it apparently.

So anyway, this is what I've been working for and here it is within days of my second anniversary here.

August 26: So what happened is I did such a good job in Irondequoit, I've been "chosen" to break in new suburban territory . . . DAMN! I've been promised three months only. If it shows signs of being more than that, I'll leave.

September 12: I keep thinking of all the people at the paper doing jobs they don't really like because those jobs offer them security or hopes of landing something they do like—all the people stuck in a rut. And I wonder if I'll have the nerve, the confidence to start over somewhere else in three months if it doesn't work out here. I just don't want to be caught in the whirlpool of forever being forced into things that don't really lead anywhere, an endless series of "what the company wants" with the faint hope that someday it will be "what you want." This would be total defeat—a silent concession that I'm not capable of doing—or afraid to trust my capabilities for—what I want to do. To me, this is a worse failure than to have tried and not measured up.

November 14: My suburban sentence ended (again) in mid-October. . . . Since the (political) campaign ended, I have had nothing to do. The various editors keep asking what story I have coming and I keep telling them I don't have any responsibilities that would produce any. Finally, today, it's beginning to get through to them.

January 23, 1967: Work is good—better than I could have expected, unless I've completely fooled myself. Since early December I've had the county government beat. The work is good and is beginning to be rewarding.

(1982 note: Comments for the next several years skipped some work milestones. If memory serves, these were among them:

(—The county government assignment just discussed had been for a couple of months while the beat reporter did a "local boys at war" tour of Vietnam. Upon his return, my assignment was made "permanent" and he set out to develop what then was called the "poverty beat."

(—My goal for the beat was to learn the county money planning and flow so well the budget process would become public. My third year on the beat, the administration and party in control gave up fighting projections of spending and taxing and all the other pieces and moved the budget cycle into the two months ahead of elections rather than the ten days after.

(—I also turned down opportunities to transfer to the city hall beat—which I backstopped anyway—and to the suburban editing desk.

(—Late in the summer of 1971, I accepted the political beat, giving up the county government after four and a half years.)

The journal resumes:

April 26, 1972: At work no one tells me what to do—but when I do things, nothing happens with them. When I offer suggestions, no one responds. When I don't do anything, no one seems to care.

The journal stops there. Much of what it reports of the years between reads like garbage anyway—lots of soap opera stuff about social life's ups and downs, few of the professional milestones.

However, stacking that against the bio sheet does tell what it was like in the 1960s and early 1970s to be young, ambitious, bright—and a single female in places populated mostly by males, men who were just discovering that women could talk about the topics that helped them earn their livings.

One undated entry, slipped in on a separate sheet, says it:

"The whole problem is that I don't know whether I'm a good reporter because I'm a sexy broad that people confide in hoping to gain favors or because I'm a good reporter who happens to be a woman."

(That entry actually was a letter I wrote but never mailed to the man who eventually became my husband. He then was a Roman Catholic priest—clearly off limits for this casual midwestern Methodist—involved in community organizing.)

Shortly after the last dated journal entry, I was assigned to fill in on the editorial page. The tryout was a huge success. Soon thereafter, I accepted the editorial page editor's proposal that I transfer from news. I didn't want to leave reporting, but the opportunity to work for a boss eager for my ideas and help had appeal.

The deal with the editor was that I'd move after the fall's election campaign and vacation. The deal with myself was that I'd recover from the ego blows for six months, then start job hunting.

Within five months, acting editorial page editor. Three months later, editor. And eight months after that, editor, publisher and president of the *Saratogian*. A year later, engaged. One month after the wedding, into the national presidency of Women In Communications, Inc. A month after passing on the gavel, promoted to publisher and president of the *Commercial-News*.

The time span from moving to the editorial page until my arrival in Danville was less than four years—January 2, 1973 to November 12, 1976.

Rereading the journal reminds me how much the circumstances are the same, even as the job, the challenges of the job, the years change. The male/female dichotomies are different, partly because I'm older and married, partly because the power relationships are different among executive "peers."

Similarities:

Motivation. What do you want to do and why? I started out wanting to pay back, through professional accomplishment and achievement, all who had helped me get to the point of the first job and to prove (the journal, again) to "hard-bitten old editors" that journalism graduates were acceptable.

Help. Someone to talk to. A network, we call it today. Or one or two special people. The right spouse, for instance. People from years ago you can call out of the blue and predict when they'll call back. Experts who know their job is to help you do yours. Bosses willing to gamble on someone different.

Perspective. Learn from whatever you're doing. How much did I learn about "good management" by feeling poorly managed? From recognizing that coincidences weren't, that they actually resulted from good management? How much did I learn about me by finding people to share experiences with? How much do you expect from yourself, from others, from your job, from your community?

Patience. That comes from all of the above.

Impatience. Don't stay stuck in a rut. The confidence and determination that come from recognizing a dead end and deciding to do something about it often translate into an indefinable something—or specific action—that ends the rut.

Initiative. If work doesn't use up all of you, what else can you do that will show what more you can do? First, I organized a chapter of then-Theta Sigma Phi. That led quickly to national leadership responsibilities in the organization and accomplishments that were key to my eventual promotion to my first publisher job.

Justification. My brothers and I were brought up to believe we were responsible for adding to any job something to justify the fact that we were given the job in the first place. It was not enough simply to continue or repeat what had been done by the person before or could have been done by anyone capable of following the pattern.

Trust. More people want you to succeed than want you to fail. That's extremely hard to believe sometimes.

Goal-setting. What do you want to do next and why? How are you going to convince someone to let you? Have you identified and trained a successor so the good you've added isn't lost, the other is analyzed and fixed?

So many key incidents, vivid today, aren't in the journal. The promotions. The accomplishments. The failures and frustrations. The advice. The lack of it. The fears. The satisfactions.

They relate to the kinds of things I just listed. They relate to living with all the things you expect journalists and managers to live with—too many things to do (when the product is new everyday and the whole world is the subject, setting limits is important, crucial).

Watching elected officials—executives, professionals—struggle to make decisions that to me were obvious changed the question from "Why me?" to "Why not me?"

Watching community or professional peers repeat the scenario has changed it again: WHY NOT ME!!!

Testing my analyses against those of the full-time specialist professionals helped me as a reporter. Same thing applies now, of course.

Social life frustrations pushed me to work more intensely (I usually buried nonwork concerns, rather than allowing them to distract me) and far longer hours than worked by those who had other lives than their jobs.

When I (finally!) had reasons to go home, I had to learn more about how to delegate, how to find or set limits.

Pragmatic community leaders who mentored me—an early thirties, single female—to the old boys taught me another version of trust. They trusted my bosses' judgment in sending me to run the newspaper, figured out how to make the best of it.

They also are an example of constructive response to the male/female changing relationships.

Those who have lectured, threatened and otherwise tried to intimidate are, I suspect, classic, defensive old boys. Not all were "power" people. Some simply were subscribers upset by poor delivery, who called at home and asked for "the girl" or for "Christy" even though they were total strangers.

Obviously, I don't know whether they'd have used the same tactics or whether as many would have, if all else had been the same except the gender of the publisher. I think not, however.

That suspicion comes from other evidence of nonacceptance such as achieving some constructive community roles only by using the same "old boy" tactics after years of straightforward efforts brought no results— even while age/experience male migrant executive peers automatically followed their predecessors into community service slots.

Beyond that, Danville suffered confusion over how to deal with its first nontraditional executive couple. Migrant executives were no problem; its pieces of many big companies (nearly two dozen Fortune 500s, for instance) had conditioned everyone to revolving doors.

But even today—six years later—we face questions from those who aren't comfortable with two different names, a husband who doesn't go to an easily defined job everyday, a wife who doesn't play bridge or weekday golf, who doesn't bake cookies or handle a share of the traditional volunteer busywork for community activities and institutions.

The other side, though, are the many, many in the community who felt (rightly or wrongly) that they at last had access to the publisher, that SHE would hear and understand what they had to say. In a mission charged with serving the total public, that asset cannot be underestimated.

How the new boss, first female boss, is accepted by employees at all levels obviously is another concern both of the individual and of those considering appointing her.

Other kinds of change have been happening within our business and our company as I have moved into and through my publisher jobs, so conclusions are difficult or impossible.

New bosses are going to be tested by some immediate subordinates and by others anyway. Whether more or less or longer or shorter, I simply don't know.

Moving toward participatory management, for instance, could be interpreted as "her weakness, lack of authority and confidence in her own ideas and ability to make decisions" or as HER recognition, because of how women are brought up, that many have a contribution to make.

Likewise, expecting more and better work faster can be HER trying to build her own career by being too demanding and bitchy or it can be HER recognition that we can do more than we've been asked to and have more to offer because women were brought up to see, nurture and develop potential of people.

Direct contact with "the boss." I grew up expecting the right and responsibility of talking directly with the top boss under the right circumstances. That violated most people's perceptions and protocols in the 1960s and part of the 1970s (I saw reporter peers duck down the stairs rather than take the elevator if the big boss happened to be on it). Direct contact is a priority management guideline and employee expectation today and has nothing to do with changing gender mix in executive suites.

Only one situation stands out as having clear gender-related overtones; and even then, the result might have been the same regardless.

During a union campaign to organize some of our casual, part-time help, our labor lawyer and I met with the people in the work unit involved. Afterwards, the lawyer's first comment was something like:

"I wouldn't have believed it. Did you sense the hostility directed at you by the women?"

The numbers in the vote were the same as the gender mix of the people voting. We don't know who voted how. But later, when a strike affected that group, the men worked, the women didn't.

Conversely, as Gannett's only publisher who was a woman (but not the first; that was Gloria Biggs in 1973. She moved to the corporate staff in 1975, leaving me as the only until the spring of 1977), I was offered many opportunities for newspaper industry service that many male peers would have given their eye teeth for (I don't have any eye teeth. I gave those up to the orthodontist during grade school).

Virtually every organization was looking for women to appoint to committees in those mid-1970s days. Al Neuharth's support for my WICI activities from early newsroom days, the WICI national visibility, the visibility of my job role, my own interest in learning and helping made me an easy target.

Target of opportunity or target, period.

Some of both, actually.

My key mistakes in this particular arena resulted from thinking that organization committees were supposed to accomplish something and that all members were expected to contribute. Some really are just excuses to get together. But even they can be parlayed into constructive progress, as others have demonstrated better than I.

The benefits are the same as for any other responsibility—the chance to learn and to try new ideas, to meet and work with people beyond your own company and community that you probably wouldn't encounter otherwise.

Thus, at a minimum, dozens of people have been responsible for my accomplishments—some in positive, constructive ways, others perversely.

The assignments in the camps of old boys so they'd get used to women doing straight professional jobs. Tips. Confirmations of hunches and calculations. Interventions and noninterventions. Going to work for the right company at the right time. Being ready when luck happened along (often my good luck was someone else's bad luck—the political scandal that gave me my first crack at a major beat, for instance).

Eighteen years.

Can't we get on with the mission? The public journal is a public trust.

The trust should extend to and serve the whole public. Thus, "women in. . ." is part of the mission.

I keep telling myself.

Patience.

Will the rest of us see the day when? I hope so. Most days I believe so.

The student reporting intern at the SPJ/SDX convention asked how to handle cops who get suggestive rather than cooperative. The 1982 SPJ/SDX convention.

Many (women) there offered to share possible solutions. It's too bad she—and they—had to use convention contacts to solve problems that should have disappeared years ago.

The "diversity principle," considered a key to "success" in the battle over AT&T, could, if applied to our own staffing and public trusting, make such skirmishes obsolete.

It will.

But when?

JUDITH G. CLABES

Robert Burke

Judith Grisham Clabes

JUDITH GRISHAM CLABES is editor of the *Sunday Courier & Press* (circulation 118,000) in Evansville, Indiana. She is a graduate of the University of Kentucky (1967) and a master's candidate in political science at Indiana State University-Evansville. She worked as a part-time copy editor for the *Henderson,* Kentucky, *Gleaner-Journal,* in the advertising department of the *Lexington,* Kentucky, *Herald-Leader,* and as associate editor of her college daily, the *Kernel.* She graduated from UK in 1967 as the Outstanding Woman in Journalism. As a high school journalism and English teacher in Henderson, she was named Teacher of the Year in 1970. During her teaching days, she also worked part time as a reporter for the *Evansville,* Indiana, *Courier* and as a stringer for an area television station. She became the first coordinator for the Evansville Printing Corporation's Newspaper in the Classroom program and subsequently became community affairs director for the *Evansville Press* before being named associate editor. She has won numerous state and local awards for column and editorial writing. In 1980, she was given the Outstanding Contribution to Reading Award by the Indiana Reading Association. She serves on the boards of several social service agencies and was elected to the American Society of Newspaper Editors board of directors in 1982. She is a member of the Indiana Women's Press Association, the National Federation of Press Women and Sigma Delta Chi. She and her husband, Gene, city editor of the *Evansville Press,* have two sons: Joey, 12, and Jake, 7. They live on a farm in Robards, Kentucky.

I walked into the editor's office of the *Sunday Courier & Press* on April Fool's Day, 1978, armed with this advice: "Act as if you know what you're doing. If the roof doesn't fall in, just keep on doing it."

That advice from the editor I was leaving behind, Bill Sorrels of the *Evansville Press,* was appropriate for the launching of my editorship on an absolutely appropos day. It was the closest thing to managment training I would get, and it probably served me as well.

Bill Sorrels was not the foolish one on April 1, 1978: To put the best possible face on it, I was positively ignorant of what I was getting into.

As the eldest daughter of two doting parents, I grew up blissfully unaware of the prejudices against women. My mother, Virginia Grisham, was one of the most innately intelligent, tolerant and caring women I would ever know. A woman of her time, she was a stay-at-home wife and mother, but as an individual she defied the mold. I was born when she was seventeen; four more children followed—three of them daughters. My father, Jesse, was a country boy, one of twelve children of Kentucky sharecroppers. He had to leave home to finish high school, and his belief in education as a way to improve one's station in life was one he passed on to all of us. His greatest sense of accomplishment is, perhaps, the college education all five of his children acquired.

It was against such a background that I began, never having been told there were certain things girls couldn't do, certain dreams girls couldn't dream. Maybe with all those girls, our parents didn't dare! At any rate, each of us grew up thinking she could do anything she wanted, if she were willing to work hard enough for it. And we had the role models at home as proof of that.

Marrying Gene Clabes was one thing I really wanted to do—and may be the best thing I've ever done. We were junior journalism majors at the University of Kentucky at the time, and those early years of struggling through school and establishing a home were some of our happiest. Gene went to work as a reporter for the *Evansville Courier* and I began teaching journalism and English at the high school where I had graduated four years earlier. We were at home, in more ways than one.

I have been forever amazed that there are men who have shed the shackles of their conditioning, in times when that was no small accomplishment. They are the open- and fair-minded men who have—in the most significant of ways—"opened the doors" for women. It was a fact as I was traveling along a career path in the late sixties and early seventies—and it will be a fact for many years to come—that I could not have advanced without the help of such men. Certainly, no one succeeds alone, no matter how talented. That may be especially true of women, however unfair; there simply aren't enough other women at the top yet to help us along.

I have been lucky to be living with one such man and to have worked for three others. My husband has spent our married life proving the reverse of the old adage, "Behind every successful man. . . ." He is the most unassuming, unegotistical, and unprejudiced man I know. He has certainly been my port in many a storm; he would never let me give up, even when I thought that would be the best thing to do.

The other three men were editors I worked for at the *Evansville Press.*

Much is said about the importance of mentors to women seeking positions of power, but TOO MUCH cannot be said. It is absolutely essential that a woman wanting entry into newspaper management have a male "mentor"—or several "mentors"—helping her along. My advice to ambitious women: Take a look around your newsrooms. If your superiors take no interest in you or show no inclination to help you along, get out quickly. Find another workplace where the atmosphere is more conducive to your success.

One thing is certain, however, and that is no matter how many mentors, no matter how much help she has along the way, no woman gets to the top unless she can handle the job. Ultimately, her success depends on her own sheer ability and talent. And, yes, that may be more true of women than of men.

It is unfortunately still a fact that a single woman is representative of her gender while a single man is an individual—with an ironic twist. A man's success or failure in a job is his own; he alone, as an individual, reaps the accolades or the blame. A woman manager, however, is too often viewed as representative of all women, and she feels the pressure associated with such wide-ranging responsibility. If she should fail, "all women" fail; she has proven that women are unsuited for management. Ironically, though, if she succeeds, she is still merely the exception. No man faces that kind of pressure.

I was teaching school the year before the summer our first son, Joey, was born and was looking for a change. I became the first coordinator of the Evansville Printing Corporation's Newspaper in the Classroom program later that year, an experience that allowed me to use both my teaching skills and my journalism training. I also learned more than I ever would have otherwise about the business, circulation, advertising and promotion side of newspapering.

Later, I went back to classroom teaching, but the die had been cast. The *Press'* editor, Michael Grehl, now editor of the *Commercial-Appeal* in Memphis, called to offer me the job as his first "community affairs director." It was a remarkable move, since Gene was by then his city government reporter and Grehl was breaking tradition by hiring a spouse. But Mike Grehl is not the kind to hide behind precedence when he knows what is right, and that job was right for me. I hope I'll have his strength of conviction when I need it.

At the time I took the job, Grehl told me I'd have to handle the editorial page "for a while." The "while" became indefinite, and I would never have given up that part of my job willingly. I loved it, and I learned so much about really good writing in the process. I began to offer some things I had written, and Grehl encouraged me to do more. Soon he asked me to write a weekly column—and it was a duty I performed with a passion. I loved what I was doing and was content to be doing it forever.

When Bill Burleigh, now editor of the *Cincinnati Post,* became editor of the *Press,* there I was, working for a good friend in a labor of mutual love. He expanded my duties, giving me even more control of the editorial page and offering me the opportunity to run the news operation on Saturdays. Wow! Was I in hog heaven, as we say in Kentucky. I was learning something new everyday—and loving it. But I think I taught Bill a few things, too. He is a devoted family man himself, but it was I who showed him that a devoted mother can be career-oriented, too. We still laugh about the Friday I went into labor in my office at the *Press,* gave birth that evening, then wrote for him my regular Monday column. I wasn't trying to be Superwoman in all that; I simply believed in living up to the responsibilities I had freely assumed. I still do.

When Bill Sorrels became editor of the *Press,* he broadened my responsibilities even more and gave me a title to match: associate editor. He is a gifted writer, and I learned much about the beauty of the language from him.

I'll never forget the day he called me into his office to tell me that the next phone call I would receive would bear an offer of the editorship of the *Sunday Courier & Press,* which had just become available. "Can you do it?" he asked with that boyish grin of his. "Sure, if I wanted to," I replied. "Then do it," he said. I honestly wasn't sure I wanted to; I could think of many reasons not to, none of them the right ones, but the biggest of which was that I really liked what I was already doing. Gene, who was at that time pursuing our horse business and not newspapering, was adamant: "Take it." "Take it," Bill Sorrels was saying. So I took it.

Never has anyone walked into a new job so ill-prepared for the onslaught. My resolve and sheer Kentucky stubbornness served me well. I determined at once that I wanted to be remembered as the best editor the *Sunday Courier & Press* ever had, not the best "woman editor," but the "best editor" who was a woman. I think that is an extremely important distinction.

Evansville is a rather conservative community, not the best place to do anything first. Maybe that was especially true for the first woman editor of the city's largest circulation newspaper. There was support, certainly, but there was also real hostility out there that I have never understood. Some of the phone calls and letters those first few months were more than a normal person could have taken. If I had had time to consider it, I might have cracked under the strain. But there were too many exciting challenges going on, all at the same time, that I had little time to be philosophical. When things got too tough, I'd simply go home to the farm and there would be a supportive husband and two darling little boys and, suddenly, there were no problems too big for me.

Evansville is still a community geared to a male power structure and penetrating that has been tedious. The country club would not allow me a membership in my name even though my newspaper was paying; I cannot join certain clubs that other editors have joined in order to be part of the community; the old boy network is alive and well. So, I've had to do things a little differently to be visible and to represent my newspaper in the community. I have been on a speaking circuit that hasn't let up. I may not be a member of those clubs, but I've been a guest speaker at all of them. I got involved in some social service agencies and in numerous projects, behind the scenes. It took a lot of extra time, but the concerted effort has paid off. Most of all, I've created an image of caring for a newspaper that is now a positive force in its community.

The more difficult problem was the staff. Let me explain how this system works: Evansville has three different newspapers in a joint operations agreement. The *Evansville Courier* is the locally owned morning daily; the *Evansville Press* is the afternoon Scripps-Howard daily; the *Sunday Courier & Press* is an entirely separate newspaper, owned jointly by the two daily ownerships, and has its own editor and staff—and no editorial continuity with the two dailies. I had been so busy—or preoccupied—with my own job at the *Press* that I was honestly unaware of the ongoing problems on the Sunday staff. I was remotely aware that there had been a union-organizing movement in the newsroom at one time, but the gory details had escaped me. So I was unprepared for the residuals of that bitter time. And I was singularly unprepared for what I believed to be an unacceptably unprofessional attitude from the staff in general. That attitude was intensified, perhaps, by the prospect of a woman in charge. But somebody needed to be in charge, and I was it.

Indicative of that was my initial contact with one of the paper's top editors. On my first day on the job, he came into my office and announced that he couldn't work for me. He had been there twenty years. The gist of his remarks was that he had now been passed over for the editorship for the third time—and "this time" (stress that) he got the message. So he'd be looking for other opportunities. Well, talk about your on-the-spot management training! I told him, fine, I'd simply work around him until he made other arrangements. It was a year before he left, and then not for a newspaper job. If I had it to do over, I would do it differently—and more decisively. But, honestly, I was caught completely off-guard. I have never since been so naive—or will be again.

My baptism of fire continued for some time. All I wanted—then and now—was a newspaper we could be proud of. To get that, an editor must have a professional staff—and I have that, now. Walk into our newsroom today and experience a breath of fresh air. Unfortunately, in order to get it, I was forced to disprove an old shibboleth: Women can't be editors because they aren't tough enough to fire incompetents. I'm not glad that that course was sometimes necessary, but it was a matter of survival. And I intended to survive.

I initiated a staff incentive program—monetary and other—as well as a regular evaluation procedure. With the help of some extremely supportive and capable staffers, who form the nucleus of a management team, I issued an employee handbook and local style and ethics guide. We started a weekly in-house newsletter and regular staff meetings and in-house workshops. We anchored on page one a regular in-depth, staff-produced feature; I was told it couldn't be done, but we haven't missed a week in five years. And I've never been ashamed. We started a local news section, a business section and a showcase feature section. We began to use full color on a routine basis. We reorganized the staff to get more reporters from the same numbers and streamlined the copydesk operation. We completely overhauled the appearance of the paper, right down to a spiffy new masthead. The paper today bears little resemblance to the one I inherited nearly five years ago, and I think that's a good thing.

My moment of greatest personal triumph came just a few weeks ago when I encountered a long-retired editor of one of the dailies. I had known early on that he had been one of my strongest critics. "Judy," he said, "when they named you editor I told them they were crazy. Now, I have to tell you that the Sunday paper is better than it has ever been."

I appreciated his candor. But, again, I'll never understand why anyone makes snap judgments on another's abilities—simply on the basis of gender. Why must I feel a constant drive to prove myself? Why do I feel part of a grand experiment? Why do the rules seem to be different for women than for men?

My husband must feel the same kinds of pressures. Now city editor of the *Press,* Gene must grow tired of the scrutiny that comes from being the husband of a "successful" wife. There are those who are constantly looking for the evidence of an emasculated man, a browbeaten husband, or a jealous professional—none of whom they would find in the person of Gene Clabes. The "problem" of the two-career couple—each of whom is equally capable and qualified and supportive of the other's endeavors—is an entirely new one for corporate America. But corporate policy is another thing altogether, and that chapter hasn't yet been written.

I remember when the announcement of my editorship was made. It got the usual "first woman" treatment. My oldest son, then seven, came home from school, beaming and bearing the news that all his teachers and friends were really happy about my "transformation." Well, I explained the word "promotion" to him, but I thought that he was probably more right. I, too, had expected a "transformation." After all, editors were important people, self-assured and all-knowing, aloof and untouchable. They made swift and sure decisions, never doubting the rightness of them. They weren't like me at all.

I soon realized, however, that an editor is simply an individual with a job to do—and no one editor does that job like any other single editor. The three super editors I had worked for had shown me that—each person has a style and a strength of his own. I had to learn that that applies to women, too.

I would be remiss if I failed to mention that man who ultimately made the decision to give me my job: Walter Goeltz, then president and general manager of the Evansville Printing Corporation, the office to which I report directly. Goeltz was nearing retirement when he had to find a new Sunday editor. As he tells it, my name kept cropping up as a possibility. It would have been understandable if he had taken an easier way out; he must have wondered, "Why me?" He once told me: "Judy, I'm a male chauvinist—and too old to change now." Well, we are all allowed some delusions, I suppose, but it's difficult for me to think of Walter Goeltz in those terms. He tells me today that he's glad he made the decision he did, but I often wonder if he might have preferred smoother sailing toward retirement.

So here I am, an editor. Others speak of lifelong goals. Certainly being an editor was not something I dreamed of as a child. My mother didn't read newspapers to me as I lay in a crib or anything as fanciful as that. The newspaper was always a part of the daily routine at our house, though, and one of my earliest memories is of my father, reclining comfortably in his favorite chair, reading the afternoon newspaper. That newspaper was the *Evansville Press* and when I began to consider working for a newspaper, that was the one I wanted to work for.

But lifelong goals? The only ones I can remotely identify are (1) a desire to write and (2) a drive to be good at whatever I was doing. From grade school days, I wanted to write. In the sixth grade, it was a puppet show that a friend and I put on at other schools around town. By high school, I was writing short stories, poems and a novel. I was almost always writing something, but when I wasn't writing, I was reading. My mother tells me I lived through my teen years with my nose in a good book. It was just as well, I suspect. I loved Emily Dickinson's poetry and every Jane Austen novel and Thomas Wolfe's *Look Homeward, Angel* and all Charles Dickens. I wanted to write, and I wanted to be good at it, like those writers I so admired.

It was a high school journalism teacher who directed my energies toward newspapers and during my year as editor of the high school paper my fate was sealed. From then on, I knew what I would do: I would write, and I would write for a newspaper.

Becoming an editor was simply part of the progression, as it worked out. But I cannot say that it was part of my own grand scheme, though it would certainly make a good story. I have simply followed my nose along the way and thereby spoiled the plot.

Even now, I am not willing to sacrifice the long-term satisfaction of a happy home life for the short-term rewards of a career, so I look to the future with that as my road map. I know what will keep me company in my old age, and it isn't a comfortable pension. Having it all is not easy. It works for me because my family has helped make it work. It takes the right combination of personalities and circumstances and I'm lucky to have somehow hit upon the magic formula. I suspect there are limits to the "success" one can enjoy and still "have it all." If so, I'm willing to live with the limitations. That is a decision based on my own priorities. All of us need to know what our priorities are, early on. We have to live with the results.

As I was explaining my new job to the two boys, Jake, then two, broke in: "Mom, will you just get me a glass of milk?" So Jake helped me expand my definition of editor. An editor is someone who, at home, fetches a glass of milk on command for thirsty little boys. That's priorities. That's a nice feeling.

It's also a nice feeling to be in charge—not just of a newsroom but of one's own destiny. And, right now, I feel content with both. I enjoy being in a position to recognize good work in good people—regardless of color, creed or gender. I have made a concerted effort to hire minorities, and there are just as many women on my staff as men. All bright, all capable, and all on the way up. They know they'll get a fair shake from me. It's a good feeling to be able to make a difference.

I remember a phone call my metro editor took a few weeks after I became editor. The irate caller was complaining about the weather story the past Sunday. The metro editor explained that we had a weather story on page such-and-such. The caller was not placated. "It should have been on page one," he retorted, "but that's just one of the stupid things that have happened since *that woman* took over." Well, as luck would have it, *that woman* hadn't been around to make that decision. She had broken her leg, been hospitalized and gone straight from her hospital bed to her first meeting of the American Society of Newspaper Editors—which she wouldn't have missed if she had broken her neck. In her absence, things were clicking along pretty much as they always had at the *Sunday Courier & Press*. But from that caller's point of view, no matter what happened at the *SC&P*—if he didn't like it, it would always be *that woman's* fault. Unfair? You bet. But you'll never win them all. Concentrate on the important ones.

There were times in the beginning when I was nearly afraid to answer my own phone, although I always do. I remember another phone call, this one on the morning of the aborted hostage rescue attempt. The troubled voice on the other end of the line said: "I just had to talk to someone with some sense." I was so flabbergasted that I nearly told her she had the wrong number. I didn't, and I'm glad.

I believe in participatory management as far as it can go. I believe in meetings and conferences and brainstorming sessions. I want every member of the staff—including the clerks—to feel a part of the process. I believe in letting people in on planning and then letting them in on the plans. I think the best newspapers are those produced by people who feel part of a team, who share a sense of purpose and mission. That doesn't mean we all think alike or act—or react—alike or have a stifling sameness. But it does mean we all know what we are about.

I know I can't do everything myself, as much as I'd really like to. I fight a natural tendency to do so. I delegate authority. My department heads have plenty of latitude, ample room to direct, to make decisions, to grow in their own jobs. Some require more backup than others; I know who they are. On the other hand, they know I don't like surprises. They alert me to any possible problems. They keep me informed. That's what I expect.

I have an open-door policy that, admittedly, sometimes gets the best of me. I answer my own phone, too, and I catch myself feeling that that is a full-time job. Yet, managing people—human beings—is one of the most important parts of my job. When one of my staffers says, "Do you have a minute?" I always do. When a reader has a comment or criticism, I want him to know that everybody at the *SC&P*, including the editor, is willing to listen.

I am not a workaholic. I like to think I'm organized—so organized that I can get a lot of work done in a reasonable time and get on with the rest of my life. Off-time is precious to me and I guard it jealously. I must have time away from work for my family—and me. I used to feel guilty about time "spent" doing "nothing." No more. Down-time makes me much more productive.

Yes, I take work home frequently. But it's work that can be done after the kids are asleep. Sometimes, I even break my cardinal rule about Monday, my day off, and accept a speaking engagement or schedule a meeting that can't be put off. But it must be something *I* decide is worth it; I've gotten better at saying "no" when I really want to.

My classroom teaching experience was invaluable training for newsroom management. It was much more practical than, say, the experience of political reporting and copy desk work. Teachers learn early on about the importance of motivation, discipline and organization—and about establishing authority. In a classroom of thirty-five teenagers, it's survival! But, most important, teachers learn to appreciate individual differences—and turn them to advantage. That's a skill many reporters-turned-editors never master and explains, in part, why a top reporter, taking the traditional route, is not necessarily the best editor.

It's funny how time seems to bridge so many gaps. After five years, I suppose I've settled in and the staff and community have settled in with me. I'm feeling a bit comfortable (not counting the ever-present drive to do better next time). Everyone else seems to be more comfortable, too. Either those in the community who resisted have become accustomed or resigned. Or maybe they've seen that the Sunday paper isn't going to hell in a handbasket after all.

Recently, a young reporter I hired shortly after I became editor said to me: "I can't imagine what it would be like to work for a man!"

I suppose that's progress. One step at a time.

EDITOR'S NOTE: Judith G. Clabes moved to the editorship of the *Kentucky Post* in September 1983.

Lou Tunno

LINDA GRIST CUNNINGHAM

Herman Laesker

LINDA CUNNINGHAM with features editor Jennifer Waestendick and staff writer Pat Gilbert (facing front).

Linda Grist Cunningham

Executive Editor LINDA GRIST CUNNINGHAM joined the staff of the *Trenton Times* (circulation 70,000) in New Jersey in January 1982, four months after the paper was purchased from The Washington Post Company by Allbritton Communications Company.

At that time she was executive editor of the *News* of Paterson (circulation 49,000) and the *Dispatch* of Union City (circulation 38,000), the other Allbritton dailies in New Jersey. Though she relinquished the title of executive editor at the *News* and the *Dispatch* in October 1982, Cunningham retains the responsibilities of the editorial direction of both papers.

Prior to joining Allbritton Communications in June 1981, Cunningham was assistant managing editor of the *Daily Record* in Morristown, New Jersey. During her four years at the *Record,* she also worked as wire editor and editorial page editor.

From 1975 to 1977 Cunningham worked as a reporter and copy editor for the *Roanoke,* Virginia, *Times & World News.* She was a reporter and then editor of the *Buena Vista,* Virginia, *News*, a weekly, from 1972 to 1975.

She is a cum laude liberal arts graduate of Marshall University in Huntington, West Virginia, where she was a staff writer for the *Parthenon,* the university daily.

She is a member of Sigma Delta Chi and served as president of the Blue Ridge chapter in Roanoke. Cunningham is also a member of the American Society of Newspaper Editors and serves on the Human Resources Committee. She attended the American Press Institute seminar for managing and executive editors.

She and her husband, Ed, have a four-year-old son.

As executive editor Cunningham is responsible for the overall editorial policies of the three dailies, general operations in the newsrooms and day-to-day direction of the *Times.*

I've been listening to my son grow. We have built our mother-son love affair through the glories of modern technology and the efficiency of New Jersey Bell.

From the days long before Lee could talk, I'd call his babysitter just to listen to Lee coo and gurgle and even to listen to him cry.

When he learned his first words, we shared them over the long-distance lines. At four, he's into longer conversations, full of chatter about school

47

and friends and what his father won't buy him when they stop at the store when Ed's finished with work.

Lee also is into guilt. "Mama," he asks with a tremble in his best baby voice, "are you coming home tonight? Why don't you want to have supper with me and Daddy? Why do you always have to work?"

I work because I have to work. Financially, physically, mentally and emotionally, I can't imagine not working. The three months I took off after Lee was born were the longest, least productive and, perhaps, most frustrating months of my life.

Certainly I enjoyed getting to know my son and sharing the pleasures and distractions of first-time motherhood. I could even find a certain joy in changing dirty diapers and going to the grocery store with the rest of the work-at-home mothers.

That isn't the way I want to live; but, oh, the guilt. I have only half-jokingly said that if Lee does something weird when he's thirty, it simply will be because I worked everyday (and many of the nights and weekends) of his young life.

When two or more working mothers gather, the conversation always will turn to issues of day care, balancing schedules, doctor's appointments and the big "G." We all have guilt; we all try to rationalize it away; we are all unsuccessful to varying degrees.

Most of the successful, professional working mothers are of a generation reared to believe that motherhood was woman's ultimate goal; that motherhood should come first above all. We were taught that while working was wonderful, it should come to a close after baby was born.

We have conditioned ourselves to believe otherwise, but doubts nag. I can handle easily multimillion-dollar budgets and personnel issues; Lee's trembling voice during my daily 6:20 P.M. call is almost insurmountable.

It goes with the territory. Though I know rationally I shouldn't let the pressures to be Supermom get to me, I fall victim at least once a day. The drive to be Superwife, Supereditor, Superwhatever, occasionally has me on a nonstop treadmill.

I am "driven." I can't be happy with doing an OK job; I can't even be satisfied with doing a good job. I have to do a great job. I don't like to fail at anything and I rarely accept defeat with aplomb.

That's nothing new. Fourth-grade students in my elementary school were evaluated on social skills. While I received check marks for everything else, I miserably took home a big, black "X" on the line item "accepts unavoidable situations gracefully."

I've tried to get better at that, the specter of Mrs. Smith and her black pen looming always in the back of my mind. While I may no longer burst into tears at minor frustrations, I feel the same churning inside.

I have to win. A male co-worker told me a couple of months ago he was convinced that any woman in a position of power was driven by an obsession to win.

"You don't know how to lose," he said with a rather snide grin. "You women never competed in sports, so you never learned how to fail. You always have to win."

He considers that a major hindrance for female managers, yet admits he, too, is driven to win. "What's good for the proverbial goose . . . ," I responded, but he'd have no part of such an argument.

That's the trauma and triumph for female managers. We have to succeed; we cannot fail. We are not, repeat, are not, anything like our male counterparts. It is not enough that we get the job done; we must get it done well. And keep house. And be mother. And. And. And. . . .

We have so much more to lose. We can tell ourselves over and over that it's OK to fail, but we can't. If I am not the best newspaper editor, it's because a woman can't do as good a job as a man. If I don't make it to the parents-teacher conference at 7 P.M. because of a meeting at work, I'm a failure as a mother because I put work before family.

We have little choice but to strive to be Wonder Woman if we want to handle daily responsibilities, but we can reach decent compromises.

Those compromises range from ridiculous to sublime, from simple to significant.

For instance, my husband and I only clean house when we know the real estate agent is coming (we're trying to sell our house so we can move closer to my work, a three-hour round trip now).

I spend one or two nights each week away from home, but I jealously guard my weekends. It must be a major issue before I'll go to the office on Saturday or Sunday.

I also take my home phone off the hook. My staffs understand that if they call me and get a busy signal, they should call back twenty minutes later. If it's still busy, they may assume I am unavailable for at least an hour.

Yes, that's a dangerous practice, and yes, I'm purchasing an answering machine, but in all the years I've done it, I have yet to miss a really important call. The people who work for me can make decisions as well as I can, and in some instances, better. If it's an issue that must have my attention, it's unlikely it can't wait an hour or so.

That hour or two the phone is off the hook guarantees me and my family that we have time alone for just us. No professional, no parental, no social, no commercial interruptions.

Little is spontaneous in my life now. That's one of the major concessions I've made because I want to be mother and wife and working woman. When the day begins at 5 A.M. and concludes at midnight, I have no choice but to plan darn near everything I do.

That's why I always have lists: grocery lists, appointments lists, "must do" lists. Not a day begins without a list and not a day ends without that list having been revised a dozen times.

But without those lists, I'd forget my father's birthday or Lee's dentist appointment or the board meeting at 11 A.M. on Tuesdays.

How often I am tempted to jump in the car and head for the shore just to listen to the ocean's roar. How soothing to the psyche to contemplate nature's wonders without a phone ringing or a staffer asking, "Do you have a minute?"

I gave up the spur-of-the-moment walks along the shore. But occasionally I'll shut my office door, put up a sign that says, "Linda is out," and just make my lists. I'll put on a Beach Boys tape instead of listening to the all-news radio stations when I'm driving in to work. I'll read cheap, romantic fiction while I brush my teeth.

I'm lucky; my husband is supportive. Ed not only gives lip-service to the idea that men should help out at home, he actually takes more than half of the homemaking and child-rearing responsibility.

Ed put it this way shortly after we were married: "I took care of myself, bought groceries and did laundry when I was single. Why should I stop now?" He hasn't and I'm grateful everyday.

Ed and I have warped Lee's perceptions of the traditional household. When he was barely able to walk, Lee followed his father around during housecleaning chores. When on one Saturday, I went for the vacuum cleaner, Lee began crying and saying "no, no." When asked what was wrong, he told me the vacuum cleaner was Daddy's and I couldn't use it. Now that's a liberated household.

Certainly there are compromises, but I believe I have the best of all worlds. I have a career I love, a family who shares the good and bad with me and a supportive bunch of friends and co-workers who share the daily grind.

I've spent many inches here talking about my personal life, deliberately placing work behind it. I felt this was appropriate, first, because whenever possible, I put my family before work and, second, there is no way I can separate my personal life from my career.

At thirty-two I am doing what I hoped to do at forty-two. I've been at the right places at the right times during the years. I've been willing to take risks to advance my career and I've had the support I needed to hold it together.

As a card-carrying Presbyterian, I believe that God has a purpose for my life. There are those who have shunted their religious beliefs, but for me, there have been too many times when only my faith sustained me. The golden rule has stood me in good stead when I made decisions that affected the lives of my staffs, and a prayer often has given me the strength to handle the sometimes overwhelming crises of the day.

I'm one of the lucky ones.

The dolls and ragged teddy bear were lined up around the room. Pencils and paper were stacked, ready for use. Teacher arrived. Class began and so did the seeds of my career.

I was six and knew I would be a teacher. I always wanted to be a teacher; I just didn't know then that teachers aren't restricted to schools or that journalism would be my medium. In 1972, I had a degree in secondary education and a teaching certificate in my hands. I peddled my diploma to half a dozen school districts in Virginia, certain I'd fulfill my dream and put my education to work.

But in 1972 no one wanted a secondary education teacher with a major in English. In fact, no one really wanted new teachers at all; the market was glutted.

Six months after graduation I was unemployed and prospects were dimming. I was searching the classifieds for behind-the-counter jobs, anything that might put some cash in my pocket and pay the bills while my first husband slugged it out in law school.

The duty of a good law-wife, according to the credo of the organization, is to provide the supportive atmosphere necessary to ensure her husband does well in school. That means, or so the credo goes, baking cookies for late-night studying, rubbing his back when he's tired, putting on a smiling facade, even when things are tough.

It also meant attending the dean's wife's annual get-acquainted tea. Remember, in 1972, I was trying to be a good law-wife. I went.

That was the first in a long series of "being in the right place at the right time" that marks my career in newspapers.

Halfway through the tea, Moonie Etherington announced she was leaving her job as a reporter for a weekly newspaper in a neighboring town. Her boss, she said, was searching for a replacement, was there anyone in the room who might be interested?

Never known as shy and retiring, I jumped up, shouted, "I'll take it!" across an embarrassingly silent parlor and presently was employed full time for the queenly sum of $52.60 a week.

I stayed with newspapers, even to the point of refusing a school job at twice the salary two years later. There is more than a little truth in the cliche about printer's ink in the blood.

I wish I had lots of funny stories to tell about my career. I wish I had anecdotes about sex discrimination, about a bitter struggle climbing the ladder to the spot of executive editor.

I wish I felt I'd paid my dues, both to the profession and to the feminist "cause."

I have few such feelings; no such stories. Newspapers and magazines don't write much about women like me because we don't make "good" copy. We don't have the heart-rending sagas to tell about how the boss offered to become a bedmate in exchange for a boost up the corporate ladder.

I believe I have talent. I've worked hard, and I've been in the right place at the right time at most of the key points in my career. My bosses have been willing to give me the shots at promotions, not because I was a woman or in spite of being a woman, but because they thought I could do the job.

So has it all been peachy keen? Not by a long shot. Instead of long stories, I'll give you two words: hard work.

Why else am I an executive editor?

I'm a bargain. Hire me and the corporation gets: (1) enough experience and ability to ensure the job will get done; (2) enough inexperience to ensure it won't have to pay top dollar; and (3) a woman who can be dressed up and taken out in public to ensure recognition of equal opportunity employment hiring.

When I presented that scenario to one of my bosses during a heated discussion on women's rights, he denied the thought had ever crossed his mind. Yet, if I were doing the hiring, I must admit I'd be thinking that way.

There are nowhere near enough women in management positions on newspapers, particularly on larger dailies. While management has a responsibility to hire the best person, we have done a lousy job getting women into management positions.

A year ago, when I looked around the news meeting table at the *Trenton Times* staff I had inherited, I was struck by the absence of women.

Of the ten editors at the meeting, I was the only woman. It was a strange situation and one we have corrected. Now there are at least four women, in addition to me, who hold key positions at that daily news meeting.

I don't have all the answers, but let me pose some of the questions:

Why aren't more of us there? Why are so few of us sitting in chairs of authority? Why do we have to smile when we'd rather scream? Why do we feel compelled to give in when a man wouldn't? And why should we have to live with the guilt society helps create for us when we put work before family?

And perhaps the most important question: Why do women have to work twice as hard to prove they can do the job? Why do we have to be Wonder Women?

There are at least two women working for me in key management positions who probably would never had been in those positions had I not been the executive editor.

Over the years both women had been passed over several times for promotions. Both are extremely talented, highly professional, and superbly motivated editors. They were the ones who always were willing to take on the jobs no one else wanted or to cover for a male supervisor who had something else to do.

But they couldn't win the promotions or the titles that went along with them. As I have worked with both women and watched them in action, I have been able to reach only a single conclusion: They were discriminated against simply because they didn't fit the mold their male bosses had set for women.

They don't "look the part." Since I couldn't care less that they don't look as though they could model for Calvin Klein jeans, I promoted both and they have never let me down.

The law student who was my first husband never accepted the drive that required me to combine career and family. For five years I struggled to be both Wonder Wife, as he required, and Wonder Journalist, as I required.

In the long run, we killed the marriage. The last couple of years were marriage in name only because I refused to accept as my own dream a house in the suburbs, a mink coat, 2.3 children and cocktail parties on the weekend.

My career was vital in helping me get through some very troubled times in the early 1970s. Without it, I might have given in to the urges that sometimes made me want to plunge from the Maury River bridge over which I drove each day to work.

The office became a place to hide; successfully completing an assignment gave me the positive stroking I craved. I put my work first, something for which a man is applauded, a woman chastised. I thought I could do it all; I couldn't. I wanted to be Wonder Woman and I failed.

He passed the bar exams; I moved on to a daily newspaper. The marriage dissolved. Professionally I was doing great; personally I was a wreck.

The move to the daily was another case of being in the right place at the right time. A couple of months earlier, I had worked on a Virginia Press Association committee with the executive editor of the *Roanoke* (Virginia) *Times & World News.*

At that time I'd told Ben Bowers I was interested in working for a daily, but added that the only position I wasn't interested in was in the women's department.

He said he'd keep me in mind. When Ben called several months later, just at the time I'd accepted the fact my marriage was completely on the rocks, the job he offered me was in the features department, and, yes, it would mean writing brides and engagements in addition to general assignment copy.

It was a take it or leave it proposition with no guarantee that anything better might open. I took it, moved out and never regretted either decision.

What followed were two years of indulging my penchant for working eighteen hours a day and partying most of the night. I consciously set aside one weekend a month during which I would arrive home at 7 P.M. on Fridays and not leave the apartment until 8 A.M. on Mondays.

I needed that weekend just to recuperate from the physical and mental destruction during the rest of the month. It was a great time and I gradually got my head back in order enough to believe that the failure of my marriage did not mean I had failed as a person.

I was growing professionally as well. Brides and engagements were a thing of the past; I was getting good assignments from both the features and news desks. Perhaps the greatest benefit to my career was hanging around after hours to learn how the desks operated.

I'd had quite a bit of experience editing copy, writing heads and laying out pages at the weekly, but since I had had only minimal guidance there, the daily was a real training ground. I'd found my niche.

Then I chucked the whole thing for a man. Ah, hah, chided my friends. You're the one who has been on the soapbox for years, hollering about how women deserve to get ahead. About how women are just as good as men. And now you're going to get married again? How dare you not be a symbol for women's rights? How dare you turn tail and do the traditional thing?

I almost gave in, that's how much guilty pressure I was willing to accept. But a veteran women's editor solved it.

"I am almost ready to retire," she told me one day during a rare personal discussion. "I have had a great career, one I have been very happy in. But when I go home at night, I go home to my cats and a solitary dinner. Do you want that when you are sixty?"

I left Roanoke in April and hit the job lines in New Jersey. It took almost two months before I found a job and when I did it was as the *Daily Record* wire editor on the lobster shift.

A newlywed, I got up at 2 A.M. to start my 4 A.M. shift. I never made it home before 2 P.M. because after I did the wire pages I had to write the editorials and lay out the edit page.

I spent nine months on that shift before I gratefully accepted a dayside position as assistant managing editor for administration. It was a great job for learning how to untangle the bureaucracy of a newsroom, how to develop personnel programs and how to wheel and deal office politics. Here I laid the groundwork as a teacher who is a journalist—from training copy editors to informing readers, it all boils down to teaching.

And then I was pregnant.

I can chuckle about this now and at the time it didn't appear to me to be the slightest bit unusual, but I'd never recommend to another woman what I did.

I continued to work full time while I was pregnant, which meant I routinely was putting in ten to fifteen hour days. At 7 P.M., Friday, November 3, I completed the newsroom budget for 1979. On Saturday, November 4, Ed and I moved lock, stock and barrel (lots of them) into our new house.

At midnight we had a cup of tea and went to bed in the only piece of furniture in the house that was in place. At 3 A.M., we were on the way to the hospital.

Lee arrived at 3 P.M. Sunday, and Monday morning I was on the phone to my secretary to juggle my schedule since I had planned to work another week.

I took three months "off," but took Lee to the office with me at least three days a week. He slept on my desk while I kept up with my newsroom responsibilities.

I found the world's greatest baby sitter through the classified ads and Lee has been with her in the daytime ever since. Elsie and her family have provided Lee with the home environment, complete with dog, cat and parrot, that he might have missed otherwise.

With the constant support of my husband and the knowledge that Lee was well cared for, I plunged back into the demands of my career. When several editors at the paper left for other positions, I took on the duties of assistant managing editor for news, while maintaining the administrative responsibilities.

It was a bear of a task, particularly since I had to shift my hours to 4 P.M. to midnight. I wasn't leaving work much before 3 A.M., which meant that with Lee getting up at 7 A.M., I was getting less than four hours of sleep a day.

I worked that grueling schedule for nine months before the phone rang with the voice of redemption.

"Mrs. Cunningham, this is John Buzzetta," the voice said. "You probably don't know me, but I am publisher of the *Paterson News*. Our executive editor is leaving and I was wondering if you might be interested in the position."

You could have knocked me over with a deep breath. Though it has been explained to me several times, I'm still not sure of the sequence of events that prompted John's call to me. Nevertheless, I figured I had little to lose by simply having a free meal and some conversation.

What John offered me was a super challenge. As executive editor of the *News* in Paterson and the *Dispatch* in Hudson County, two of the three papers owned by Allbritton Communications Company in New Jersey, I would have the chance to put into practice everything I believed about newsroom management. That, plus a pay raise and a good title. How could I refuse? I considered doing so. The *News* and the *Dispatch* had been plagued by labor strife, including a strike. Neither paper was known for substantial financial wherewithall, but both were considered decent newspapers.

I couldn't resist the challenge. During the months, I hired two managing editors, Maureen Gibbons Urbanowitz at the *News* and Joe Ruda at the *Dispatch*. Together we built two solid newsroom staffs, improved the papers' responses to their respective communities and generally got on with producing good newspapers.

Nine months later I received another call, this time the voice of "do-I-have-a-surprise-for-you." It was Dean Singleton, vice-president of Allbritton Communications and president of the *Trenton Times*. Could I come to Trenton that day?

I switched around my schedule and headed south. In late January 1982, I took on the rebuilding of the *Trenton Times* newsroom, which had been bought from The Washington Post Company by Allbritton Communications Company in November 1981.

When Walt Herring joined the staff as managing editor in April, we got down to the serious issues of news direction, staff rebuilding and development and community involvement.

Nine months later we can point to successes we never thought would arrive. Where once there was overt hostility, there is laughter; where once the community was tossing over the paper in favor of the other morning newspaper, they are coming back.

Why? The successes of all three papers I attribute to my belief that chicken dinners and what journalists call "major news" carry almost equal weight. We care about things big and small in our readers' lives. We let our readers know what they want and what they need.

I've given up the day-to-day responsibilities for the *News* and the *Dispatch,* since Maureen and Joe are more than capable of taking care of business. That alone is proof that I've begun to learn I don't have to do everything by myself, that I don't have to be Wonder Woman.

I love my job; I won't imagine what my life would be like without the printer's ink. Each day I learn a little more about balancing my work and my family—both involve my love of people.

And I'm buying an answering machine so when I call home and Ed and Lee aren't there, I can leave a message for my two favorite people.

KATHERINE (KAY) FANNING in March 1981 with the first edition of the new Sunday *Anchorage Daily News*.

On the day of the Pulitzer Prize announcement in May 1976: KAY FANNING with Jim Babb, Bob Porterfield and Howard Weaver, the reporters for the winning series, "Empire: The Alaska Teamsters Story."

KAY FANNING outside the new *Anchorage Daily News* plant.

Katherine Woodruff Fanning

KATHERINE WOODRUFF FANNING grew up in Joliet, Illinois, and received her B.A. from Smith College in 1949. She lived in Chicago following her marriage in 1950 to Marshall Field, Jr. until, after a divorce, she moved to Alaska in 1965 with three children, Katherine, Barbara and Frederick Field.

In 1966 she married Lawrence S. Fanning, a former editor of the *Chicago Sun-Times* and the *Chicago Daily News*. A year later, the Fannings purchased the *Anchorage Daily News*, a small-circulation morning newspaper then barely surviving in the shadow of the much larger afternoon *Anchorage Times*. For the next four years, she assisted her husband in every aspect of the newspaper operation, serving as reporter, Sunday magazine editor and advertising salesperson.

After Mr. Fanning's death in 1971, she assumed editorial direction and management of the *Daily News*. After an unsuccessful joint publishing agreement with the *Times*, she sold an eighty percent interest in the *Daily News* to McClatchy Newspapers of Sacramento, California. She continues as editor and publisher.

Since April 1979, the *Daily News* has grown from a circulation of 12,000 to the current 32,000. On February 1, 1981, the newspaper launched a Sunday edition.

The *Daily News* won a Pulitzer Prize "Gold Medal" for meritorious public service in 1976 for an investigative series describing the growth and power of the Alaska Teamsters Union. It was a project conceived and directed by Mrs. Fanning. Other recent awards for the paper include the Associated Press Managing Editors public service award, two Headliner Awards from the Atlantic City (New Jersey) Press Club, and the Alaska Press Club public service trophy for six consecutive years.

Mrs. Fanning serves on the Alaska Education Broadcasting Commission, the boards of the Alaska Repertory Theatre, the YMCA, the Anchorage Chamber of Commerce and as president of the United Way. She is a member of the Alaska Press Club, Sigma Delta Chi, the American Society of Newspaper Editors (board of directors), the Pulitzer Prize Board, and the Alaska Newspaper Association.

In 1979, she was the recipient of the Elijah Parish Lovejoy Award at Colby College, which included an honorary Doctor of Laws degree; and in 1980 she received the Smith College Medal and the Missouri Medal of Honor given by the University of Missouri Journalism School.

Our 1963 Buick station wagon, bulging from roof to axles, had just

59

plunged into a ditch deep in the Yukon Territory. The three children and I stood ankle deep in mud surveying the damage. It was a watershed moment. What were we doing here far from our Illinois roots? Should we give up this whole crazy idea of moving to Alaska? Eleven-year-old Kathy and eight-year-old Barbara began to cry while their brother Ted struggled to be manly. "Oh dear, Mommy," sniffled Barb, "now we're going to have to walk to Alaska."

I began to laugh and seized the movie camera to record the scene. Soon an old couple in a camper stopped to help and so did another car and then another. Within an hour we were again bumping our way north through the Alaska Highway's heavy gravel.

My route to becoming a newspaper editor was as circuitous as the twisting Alaska Highway. Until that summer of 1965 my adult life had been largely spent as a conventional wife and mother. I had had it easy growing up as an only child with two adoring parents in a rambling ranch house outside Joliet, Illinois—a solid but uninspiring blue-collar city forty miles from Chicago. My father was the third generation in a line of bank presidents, but he was also an exceptional human being—much traveled, full of adventure and humor—who was loved in the town because of his caring attitude toward his customers and the community. He started talking to me about issues like the Russian five-year plan when I was six and always treated me as if there were no limitations on what I could do or be, despite my age or sex.

My mother was a southern belle who grew up in Louisville, a red-haired beauty who was still dancing on her eightieth birthday. Mother reveled in being a woman. My father inspired me with interest in the things men talked about.

Both made me feel special, so special I went to school in my own house with nine other children through sixth grade, then was driven thirty miles every day to school through junior high. Longing to escape this isolation, I was allowed a year at the Joliet high school before being shipped off to a strict eastern girls boarding school where I spent four miserable years unpopular and convinced of my own mediocrity. Failure to achieve any sort of distinction during those high school years probably contributed to a lifelong empathy with the underdog, perhaps a useful bent for a newspaper person.

The unsatisfactory outer life in boarding school also turned me toward study and the cultivation of an inner self. I did a major project on eastern religions and settled on a religious commitment of my own (Christian) that was to support and guide me through the travail ahead.

By the time I reached Smith College, ideas germinated during the lazy Joliet summers of my childhood had begun to take root—that most other people were not as fortunate as I and that I owed society a positive contribution. Majoring in English literature, I took every writing course the college offered as well as reporting occasionally for the alternative college newspaper (I have always had an attraction for No. 2 newspapers), writing a play that was later produced, co-authoring and producing two musical comedies and shepherding one of them to a double-truck spread in *Look* magazine.

Although I dreamed of a New York magazine career, my mother persuaded me to return to Chicago, join the Junior League and behave like a Chicago society woman—thus delaying the life I really wanted for another fifteen years.

A year after graduation I married Marshall Field, Jr. (of the department store family) who soon became editor and publisher of his father's newspaper, the *Chicago Sun-Times.* The *Sun-Times* was decidedly the No. 2 morning paper in Chicago behind the *Chicago Tribune* and in that year, 1950, it was also a substantial money loser. But within three years Marshall had made it profitable, greatly improving its quality.

I was closely associated with this effort behind the scenes, a once-removed education in all aspects of a metropolitan newspaper. Marshall brought home his journalist associates, and also his problems which we would work on together. He would never consider my taking an active role in the newspaper or having a career of my own. So I served on charitable boards, enjoyed my children and traveled with my husband.

Because Marshall was never really comfortable with the downscale tabloid format of the *Sun-Times,* I encouraged him in the acquisition of the respected afternoon *Chicago Daily News* which was accomplished in 1959.

The newspaper business was a major bond between Marshall and me. Much of my idealism about a newspaper's potential for good came from him.

But by 1963 the marriage was falling apart and I was increasingly dissatisfied with the isolation of the cloistered society matron. There was a divorce, followed by two transitional years living with the children in Chicago's Old Town area, carefully removed from the wealthy Gold Coast. It was a time for involvement with the civil rights movement, the Council on Foreign Relations and the Great Books; a time for self-examination and despair. I felt my life was like a runaway cable car on a San Francisco hill—out of control. Now was the time to arrest the descent, if it was ever to come at all.

I briefly considered self-destruction, but the inner spiritual self developed during my boarding school years emerged and took charge. Within a few months I had thrown out tranquilizers and sleeping medicines, stopped smoking and drinking and begun to rebuild.

Two years after the divorce, pulling out of the ditch in the Yukon Territory, I was high on the prospect for adventure. I was also intent on living in the real world, having escaped the insulation experienced by families with a prominent name and eager to make some useful contribution in the new land—"America's Last Frontier" as the increasingly frequent Alaska license plates declared it.

When we arrived in Anchorage in August 1965, the city was still sorting out the rubble left by the great Alaska earthquake a year earlier. Our barely completed white clapboard house was on an unpaved street and there was a six-week wait for a telephone. Winter came quickly, the paving machines just ahead of it as they crept up the street in the dark while huge flakes began to fall in October's first blizzard. The asphalt was still steaming as it was smothered in snow.

Anchorage was a fairly civilized little western town in that year. It had two hotels and a J. C. Penney's store that had already been rebuilt since its destruction in the earthquake. The one small shopping center boasted the only escalator in town—in a department store called Caribou's.

But it had two newspapers. One was the 30,000-circulation, firmly established *Anchorage Times* owned by the Atwood family. The other was the tiny 8,000-circulation morning *Anchorage Daily News* which had been started by Norman Brown and his wife Blanche. Brown, a former *Anchorage Times* editor, founded the paper as a weekly in 1946, converted it to an afternoon daily the following year and later moved it to morning publication, adding a Sunday edition. It occupied a dingy warehouse in the industrial section of town where it was produced on antique equipment and written by a news staff of eight.

I promptly went to work for the *Daily News* as a $2.00 an hour librarian. My job was to sort through cardboard boxes full of clippings, photo prints and negatives from which I was supposed to develop a library. It was tedious work in a stuffy room next to the noisy Associated Press radio wire, the only wire service then available. But it was a good way to learn about Alaska, a task I relished.

One day my daughter Kathy brought home a friend from school whose father was a local doctor. His name was Ivey and I discovered he was the son of the notorious Doctor Ivey then on trial in Illinois for illegally selling the drug Krebiozen, a discredited cancer remedy. My interview with Ivey made page one of the *Anchorage Daily News*. Suddenly I was a reporter.

Never having learned to write a news story, I read other newspapers and tried to copy the style. When I was assigned to cover the deaths of three university students who had frozen during a field trip on a glacier just a few miles from Anchorage, I said to myself, "You don't know how to do this. Just let the story tell itself." The glacier story won first place in the spot news category at the annual Alaska Press Club awards banquet (I suspect there were very few entries) and I was awarded the best series prize for some pieces I had written on the problems of promoting birth control among Natives in the Alaska Bush. The series grew out of a simple feature assignment but the subject warranted in-depth treatment, so I got up at 3:00 A.M. to write on my own time. The story caused quite a stir when it appeared on page one, illustrated by a photo of a large hand holding a contraceptive, on the day Alaska's first Roman Catholic Archbishop arrived in Anchorage.

Certainly I hadn't become a trained reporter by this time. But in the Alaska of the sixties you could break into the newspaper business, or any business, with the appropriate mixture of curiosity, enthusiasm and gall. I never would have dared to try it in Chicago.

What I loved most about Alaska, besides the glory of its mountains and the glittering winter snow, was the warmth of its people. In Alaska no one seemed to care who you had been or what you had done before you migrated north. Total equality. A classless society. A chance to begin again. I liked that.

Firmly in love with my new state, I returned to Chicago with the children the following summer and married Larry Fanning, who had edited the *San Francisco Chronicle, Chicago Sun-Times* and *Chicago Daily News*. He had launched the careers of a variety of prominent journalists, among them Ann Landers, Mike Royko and Nick Von Hoffman. After separating from Field Enterprises, Larry returned with me to Alaska to sell my house and bring me back to "civilization." But he too was soon captured by the magnetism of Alaska and, against all the advice we sought, in the fall of 1967 we bought the *Anchorage Daily News* from the Browns.

I had my hands on a newspaper at last. Larry was the editor and publisher. I did a smattering of everything—reporting, writing a column, selling ads, even running the accounting department in an emergency. I edited our low budget Sunday magazine, Alaska Living, writing most of the pieces, doing the layout and producing it. During the first weeks Larry, a perfectionist, would often keep me at the paper until three or four in the morning writing and rewriting headlines and cutlines—occasionally to the point of tears. Then we would drive home through an empty Anchorage at 4 A.M., each in our own cars, side by side. A few blocks from the house I would drop behind him and follow his red Volkswagon home. We never discussed it but it symbolized our relationship—which was mostly side by side. Sometimes I dropped back, sometimes he did.

As a journalism teacher Larry was superb. He could mold green college students into reporters. He saw the *Daily News* as a laboratory newspaper where young journalists could spend a couple of years before returning to larger newspapers in the "Lower 48" and where he could test new journalistic concepts—often years ahead of other newspapers. I was as raw as any of the kids we hired and I envied those with enough training to know what a pica was.

Our cramped newsroom and business department was in the front of a warehouse that housed the seventy-five-year-old museum piece we used for a press. It was later replaced—with much pride—by a "new" Goss Tubular, a thirty-year-old anachronism with thousands of moving parts. We had six linotypes and an array of Alaska characters who served as printers.

We were an intense and tightly bound little force that put out the *Daily News* from the warehouse on Post Road. The financially precarious paper always hovered on the edge of oblivion as the deficit mounted. The Browns had kept the only profitable end of the business, a commercial printing operation. All our equipment was obsolete and had to be upgraded. And, worst, it became increasingly difficult to attract advertising. Larry and I had ingenuously taken editorial positions that were anathema to most Alaskans, notably our editorials advocating gun control in a place where almost everyone owned at least one gun.

During the late sixties Alaska's Eskimos, Indians and Aleuts joined in the Alaska Native claims movement, a campaign to receive title or compensation for their ancestral lands. The *Daily News* was denounced from the podium of the Anchorage Chamber of Commerce because of our support for the Natives. Several years later (after the passage of the Native Claims Settlement Act of 1971 granted the Natives 44 million acres of land and nearly a billion dollars creating regional Native corporations in the process), we could turn to the Natives and find help in keeping the paper alive.

The discovery of one of the world's giant oil fields at Prudhoe Bay began to transform Alaska in 1968. Because we published an award-winning thirty-two part series on the potential dangers of laying an 800-mile hot oil pipeline across permafrost, we were perceived by the business community as antioil, antidevelopment, antibusiness—labels that lingered despite our eventual support for the pipeline. To the old-time Alaskans we were "cheechakos," interlopers from "Outside" who didn't properly respect Alaska's boom-bust economy. Advertisers eschewed the *Daily News* in droves and the financial crisis deepened.

Years later a prominent Anchorage banker would tell me over lunch that for some ten years he had refused loans to any client who advertised in the *Anchorage Daily News*.

The money troubles weighed heavily on Larry. He had once told me that he expected to check out of this existence with a massive heart attack in the newsroom. One February day in 1971 after a period of poor health he did exactly that—a few feet from the newsroom door.

It never occurred to me to do anything after Larry's death except continue to run the *Daily News*. I was visited by Tom Brown, our talented reporter who wrote the Oil on Ice series, and by Stan Abbott, Larry's able managing editor, who offered to do anything if only I would keep the paper going. I asked them to run the newsroom which they did together admirably for two years. I expected to stay at home at least part time with the children, but after taking them on a trip to the Soviet Union and seeing two of them off for college, I returned to Anchorage with renewed energy for the newspaper.

Soon I was in the office full time. Still, the transition was abrupt. I had been married to two editors; now I *was* the editor. At first I was uncomfortable behind Larry's big desk. Whenever a man came in to meet with me, I would sidle around the desk, pulling my chair to the side. I knew I was moving into a job usually held by a man but I had always enjoyed being a woman. I vowed to cherish my womanhood, to make it as effective and decisive as necessary but never to become like a man.

This was another time to lean heavily on the spiritual support system I had developed in boarding school and renewed at the time of the divorce. While driving to work in the morning I would say: "Okay, God, I haven't got the slightest idea what to do today . . . you'll have to show me."

A couple of months after Larry's death, Dave Stein, Larry's general manager, presented me with a brand new organizational chart he had developed. It was clear that my services would not be required under this plan for more than a couple of hours a week. He was taking over. I rejected the plan firmly. Later Dave announced that he was probably going to accept an offer to work for a real estate firm. Dependent as we both knew I was on him at the time, some angel prompted me to smile and say, "All right, Dave, if the real estate business is going to make you happy, I wouldn't dream of standing in your way." That was the last I ever heard from Dave about real estate. We worked together harmoniously for several more years.

From Larry I learned about dealing with people, especially newspeople. He literally loved his reporters and editors. He understood that talented people were special and must be treated according to their often very individual needs. He was a tremendous listener. Sometimes at the end of a day there would be a line of staffers just waiting to talk to Larry about their personal or professional problems.

It was easy for me to feel the same way about our staff. With Larry gone they were the people with whom I shared the dream of a first-rate newspaper at the top of the world, dedicated to journalistic excellence and public service. With my personal family of five now down to two, the staff became my extended family. They worked *with* me, not for me.

Later as the size of the staff grew larger than a family, I continued to think of us all working together side by side advancing toward the twin goals of survival and excellence. It often surprised me when others treated my opinions deferentially because I was the boss. My style was to look for consensus to develop, but if that failed I found I could make the tough decisions.

Sometimes that meant firing people. Early that first year I had to replace the advertising manager. To me the dignity of every individual is important so I wanted the ad manager to leave my office understanding that his performance had been inadequate but without feeling demeaned as a person. That approach has continued to work for me, in most cases avoiding the anger, hurt feelings and recriminations so often associated with letting people go.

Gradually we built a talented team in both the business and editorial departments, but the financial pinch grew steadily worse. By this time my eighteen-year-old son Ted had invested considerable trust fund money in the newspaper and his trustees urged me to approach Bob Atwood, owner-publisher of the *Anchorage Times,* about a joint operating agreement similar to those in twenty-two other cities. Although the *Times* and *Daily News* had taken opposite positions on nearly every Alaska issue (the *Times* being rigidly conservative and the *Daily News* much more liberal), a merged publishing entity seemed in the best interest of both papers and the community. The *Times* had modern offset printing equipment in a new plant while the *Daily News* equipment was obsolete and barely functioning. But the *Daily News* had the only Sunday paper in town, and so after nearly three years of negotiations a Joint Operating Agreement (JOA) was approved in late 1974 by the U. S. Justice Department. It meant that the *Anchorage Times* printed, sold the advertising and distributed the *Daily News* out of its downtown plant, but the *Daily News* gave the Sunday paper to the *Times*.

We had high hopes for the new arrangement. The agonizing worries about paying the bills would be over. We were confident that, although the agreement with the *Times* did not include profit-sharing as most such contracts did, with good management and good equipment at the *Anchorage Times* and a high quality of editorial product, the *Daily News* could become financially viable.

After moving into a new building constructed for us by the *Times* adjacent to their facility, we turned our attention to editorial excellence and public service reporting.

To me that included investigative reporting. We had tried our hand at investigation early in the Alaska pipeline buildup when there was a clear threat that free-flowing cash would attract organized crime. We began publishing stories about organized crime's attempts to move into Alaska, exposing a mob-connected corporation that coveted an Anchorage cable franchise. We ran a series on massage parlors by rookie reporter Howard Weaver, now *Daily News* managing editor. Weaver landed in jail one morning at 3:00 for trespassing in a massage parlor. His crime: He wanted to *talk* to the proprietress.

Strapped as we were for advertising revenue, when the series revealed drug dealing, prostitution and extortion flourishing in the massage parlors, we refused to accept any further massage parlor advertising. We tried to take the principled position, even if it appeared to be damaging in the short run—as it often was.

During the summer of 1975 the construction of the 8 billion dollar Trans-Alaska oil pipeline was in full swing when rumors were circulating that the Alaska Teamsters Union and its powerful boss, Jesse Carr, controlled the state through financial and political clout. We determined to uncover the truth about the Teamsters, to report what was good as well as expose what was bad about the union. Three of our eight reporters were detached for the full-time effort over a period of three months. When we were well into the project, the *Los Angeles Times* sent four reporters to Alaska searching out much the same story. Since the *Times* reporters' approach was less detailed than ours, they were ready for publication first. There was a temptation to rush our series into print before it was ready, but we refrained in order to present a complete, thoroughly documented account. A few months later we were rewarded with a Pulitzer Prize Gold Medal for Public Service—we had even triumphed over the *Los Angeles Times* which had also submitted their Alaska series. The announcement of the Pulitzer was an ecstatic experience—champagne corks popping, phones ringing, all Anchorage rejoicing with us. Alaska had never won a Pulitzer before.

But the joy was short-lived. Four months later we published a notice to our readers that the *Daily News* was deep in the red and would have to close unless there was immediate financial aid. Spreading out this dismal picture before our readers was a hard decision, but it has taught me the value of candor. The experience of going publicly broke may have been as rewarding in its way as the Pulitzer Prize. The reaction was astonishing. Over a hundred diverse citizens crowded the *Daily News* offices and formed The Committee for Two Newspapers.

The Committee's purpose was to save the *Daily News* by selling subscriptions, talking to advertisers and encouraging our efforts to secure major financing. Soon one of the Native corporations provided us with a low interest loan of $70,000 that took care of the expenses for a few months. The staff had been cut in half, from twenty-five (excluding *Anchorage Times* employees who operated the business and production departments) to twelve, including myself and an accountant. But there was no income from the revenue departments operated by the *Times* and by this time all my resources had been invested in the paper.

When the Native corporation loan ran out we faced closing again. I traveled around the country talking to individuals, corporations and foundations seeking the aid that could not be found through banks. An amazing array of people helped. Actor Robert Redford hosted a reception at his New York apartment for prospective investors. A wealthy midwestern woman backed the newspaper with a series of loans amounting to over a quarter million dollars.

Other individuals, some of whom I never met, made loans of $50,000 or more. Altogether some $750,000 was raised in this unconventional fashion from people who believed in the *Daily News* mission in Alaska. Fortunately all were repaid with interest within three years.

Meanwhile the relationship with the *Anchorage Times* was deteriorating rapidly. In the winter of 1977, I reluctantly filed a lawsuit claiming contract violations and antitrust allegations against the *Times* management of our joint operation. It was a sad necessity. I had tried to gain the attention of *Times* publisher Bob Atwood without going to court. Perhaps the fact that I was a woman was a factor in Mr. Atwood's original willingness to enter the JOA. But just as certainly it contributed to his failure to take my stewardship of the *Daily News* seriously and court became the only recourse.

Once during negotiations that led to the JOA, Bob Atwood said, with reference to my widowhood, "It's just a matter of time before some man on a white horse will gallop up and carry you away."

In a dramatic November 1977 courtroom confrontation the *Times* attempted to end the joint agreement, a move that, if successful, would have abruptly stripped the *Daily News* of publishing facilities and closed the paper. In his summation the *Times* lawyer, after cross-examining me intensely for several hours, described me as "this obsessed woman and her *little* newspaper. . . ." The judge reprimanded the attorney for his characterization and promptly ruled in our favor, a ruling that forced the *Times* to publish the *Daily News* under federal court injunction until the lawsuit was settled a year later.

Settlement came after five weeks of arbitration hearings which, although inconclusive, favored the *Daily News*. The settlement required the *Times* to pay us three quarters of a million dollars and gave us six months to establish the paper in a new plant before the end of the joint operation.

It also launched a scramble as threatening as anything we had faced before. It was quickly clear that neither the money nor the time was sufficient to create what amounted to a whole new newspaper. Frantically and unsuccessfully I scoured the country for a general manager, advertising, production and circulation personnel willing to move north to Alaska for such a risky venture. After the April 1 deadline, there would be no newspaper if the plant and personnel were not in place. With help from the Fairbanks paper to the north, I ordered a press and computer production system even though we had no plant to put it in, no personnel to operate it, and no clear idea how we were going to pay for it.

Substantial payments were due on the production equipment in mid-January. I knew that without major capital investment by that time I would have to fold the paper. At the end of December I was introduced to executives of McClatchy Newspapers, owners of the *Sacramento Bee,* and by the first week in January C. K. McClatchy and I had hammered out a deal over breakfast in Anchorage. McClatchy Newspapers would own eighty percent, I would retain twenty percent and a contract to manage the paper with complete editorial independence. Losing the controlling interest hurt, but there would be expertise, an infusion of capital and partners I could admire and trust.

After that things moved fast.

McClatchy bought us a million-dollar building on the outskirts of Anchorage a week later. By April 1, some sixty people had been hired, the computer system and press had been installed and were operating, the paper redesigned, the local news staff substantially expanded. By October, circulation had grown from 12,000 to more than 20,000 and in three more years, by October 1982, the *Daily News* weekday circulation was over 50,000, surpassing the *Times*. A Sunday paper had been re-established and advertising volume was approaching parity with the *Times*. Although the paper was not yet profitable, the trend lines were right. The *Daily News* was rapidly emerging as Anchorage's leading newspaper. Competition was still intense but the paper, marginal for years, was moving into Alaska's mainstream.

During the lawsuit years I had been virtually ostracized from social and business circles in Anchorage. The *Times* and the Atwood family were so dominant in the town, few dared invite us to occupy the same room. I never shared this antagonism—to me the lawsuit was only an attempt to resolve a stubborn business conflict, but *Times* owners took it as a personal affront. For several years members of the Committee for Two Newspapers, the newsroom staff itself and three or four friends were my only support. Again I relied heavily on that inner spiritual support system developed earlier.

As the *Daily News* began to grow and flourish in the eighties, the paper was now closer to the pulse of Alaska. Not that we had changed so much. True, we had abandoned some of our more impractical positions such as gun control, but we adhered to others like support for the environment, planning, green space, beautification and Native causes. These had become the mainstream of the eighties. Possibly we had contributed to making it so. Even the divisive battle over federal withdrawal of Alaska land for parks and wilderness had faded, and with it the acrimony.

My relationship with the community changed in other ways. When the newspaper was small I had served on commissions and boards—the Urban Beautification Commission, the Educational Broadcasting Commission, United Way—but as the paper has grown in influence, I have refused such appointments to maintain maximum independence and objectivity.

The adjustment to corporate life was a challenge in the beginning too.

The merger with McClatchy had been sudden and swift. I was no longer a sole entrepreneur. Now I answered to a boss—and the first few months I didn't do it very gracefully. McClatchy sent in a management consultant with whom I immediately tangled. She saw my management style as oppressive. I was trying to be everywhere, involved in every decision. Back off, she said, and so did my bosses. Now that someone else's investment was at stake, I was even more intensely devoted to the paper's success. Reluctantly, I did back off and learned to delegate better. The whole newsroom staff no longer fit on our "one green couch" as reporter/columnist Suzan Nightingale had described it. Now I was an editor once-removed from the news staff, responsible for the content and editorial policy of the paper but also for an ever-growing business side.

New ways of relating both up and down had to be established. After years of close association with some of our managers, whole relationships had to be reworked. What was successful during the years of struggle was no longer effective. I found I was too quick to pass out criticism, too demanding and often I forgot to encourage and compliment.

Since my work experience had begun near the top of a tiny hierarchy, I had little experience in the ranks and therefore wasn't sufficiently sensitive to the effect of the words of the boss on reporters and lower-level editors. With a newsroom staff that burgeoned from twelve to sixty and finally to 300 in a three and a half year period, there were major lessons to be learned: to delegate, to be willing to listen, to allow all levels of staff to advance ideas and take the credit, to avoid involvement with every detail, to let others take the lead in meetings and listen to their views before giving mine—and I'm still learning.

But now, nearly four years into the corporate relationship, I am enjoying the associations both up and down. If there is a single virtue that I believe is vital to women editors it is flexibility, even humility. Perhaps because we're trying to make it as women, we think we must know it all. I remember a recurring nightmare I used to have. I was dangling out of a hole in the side of a commercial airliner aloft and I couldn't communicate my plight. After a terrifying interval I finally managed to scream at the top of my lungs "HELP!" waking myself up. It's surprising how people will rush to our aid if we only ask.

Mine was a tortuous road to the "top"—if indeed that's where I am. But I do believe there is no one route to achieve that position. No one background, no one age to start, no limitation on what can be achieved by any of us. I think it's important to assess our own motivation often along the way. Am I in this purely for self-glorification? Do I simply want to enhance my own ambitions? Or is there a larger purpose? Do I believe in something more important than myself? Isn't there a vital public service to be performed in determining what the public is going to read each morning and evening? Doesn't the content of our newspapers establish the very thought structure of our community and our world? And if that is so, then it is a supreme privilege and responsibility to be an editor.

EDITOR'S NOTE: Kay Fanning was named editor of the *Christian Science Monitor* in May 1983.

Sarah Plunket

ANN FARAGHER

Melva Geyler

ANN FARAGHER in front of courthouse.

Ann Faragher

ANN FARAGHER has been editor of the *Herald Banner,* a 13,000-circulation, seven-day morning newspaper, in Greenville, Texas, since 1966. She supervises a staff of twelve.

She is a graduate of the University of Kentucky with a B.S. in home economics. She worked her way into the newspaper business circuitously, having become fascinated with the news business when she handled publicity for the local PTA. It was a fascination that would acquaint her with every facet of the business and would eventually lead to the editorship of the *Herald Banner.*

Mrs. Faragher has four children, G. W., Abbie, Phoebe, and Audrey, and six grandchildren.

She is a member of the Texas Press Women, the AAUW, the National Federation of Press Women (treasurer, 1983), and the Texas Parent Teacher Association.

In Greenville, she is a member of the Salvation Army advisory board and the Hunt County Council on Alcohol and Drug Abuse.

She has received over 100 awards for writing, photography and page layout.

If ever a newspaper editor got into this business through the back door, I am one.

When I was making my initial career plans, being a newspaper editor was not an alternative I considered. And no one was more surprised than I when I became a reporter.

My parents wouldn't let me go to nursing school to become an emergency operating room specialist. So I went to college in Kentucky and majored in science and math, thinking that with so much science behind me, I could later put myself through nursing school.

What I wound up with was a B.S. in home economics with a major in the chemistry of foods and minors in chemistry and math. And I also completed all the education courses required for a teaching certificate, except practice teaching. I thought adult education as an extension agent might be a way to get a job because there were almost no scientific openings for women. And I had vowed never to be a public school teacher because I knew I could only teach people who wanted to learn and I could not put up with public school discipline problems.

Nothing happened the way I expected.

World War II arrived and I went to work in West Virginia as an analytical chemist for a major company—the first professional woman chemist hired by that company.

In addition to preparing control chemicals for the whole plant, I got to carry out experiments I suggested in cooperation with the research department which was trying to develop a fast-color, hollow rayon cut filament to replace wool in military clothing. That led to learning micro-photography—projecting slides through a microscope onto photographic paper—so the researchers could study the air-trapping capabilities of their fibers. And that led to learning camera use and darkroom procedures. All of this involved report writing and detailed records.

War years being unsettled, I moved two years later to Pennsylvania to be with my husband at a Navy base—where he had been told he would be stationed for two years—and landed a job with the Navy. I started as a clerk in the Spare Parts Distribution Center where we directed replacement and emergency shipments for the internal combustion engines of the U.S. Navy and all the Allies. My husband was sent to the South Pacific two months later.

Within a year I was supervising eight civilian clerks and ten sailor and WAVE clerks; had been cleared for handling classified documents; and monthly, manually reviewed the three-inch thick IBM printouts directing replacement spare parts shipments around the world.

Some of the errors I found and corrected were pretty big. One month, the printout ordered replacement camshafts for three times the engines of a particular brand which were in service. Another month thousands of parts for a specific engine were directed to Alaska when all craft with those engines had been moved to the South Pacific.

I also spent hours on the telephone tracking down lost shipments and getting the emergency spare parts on the move again.

So far, nothing looks like newspaper.

After the war, my husband, son and I moved to the West Coast and my son started first grade in February 1947. Naturally I went to PTA meetings. After all, some of my earliest memories were of going to PTA meetings with my school principal father and my mother.

The new PTA president elected in May asked me to be publicity chairman and I was persuaded to accept after she told me PTA had a wonderful handbook that tells you exactly what to do. I knew I had a good command of the language and grammar and I had always earned excellent ratings on my written reports, both in school and at work.

I had taught myself to knit, crochet, sew and cook from how-to books and I thought publicity work could be learned from a book just as well. I was right, but it wasn't as easy. My other self-teaching had involved only myself. Publicity involved outside forces, cooperation from others and coordination of multiple activities. Such a challenge!

To tell the truth, my brain had been working only slightly over idle speed in the ten months since I had left my Navy job to become a full-time housewife for the first time in my life. Of course, I had shiny floors, good meals, white collars, and my craft classes. But didn't everyone?

Publicity chairmanship was, I thought, an excursion into an unplowed field for me. The PTA handbook taught me about the multiple means of publicity of which I had never dreamed—newsletters, posters, bulletin board notices, notes sent home with students, radio bulletin boards, interview opportunities, newspapers and DEADLINES. Television was an infant and even the PTA hadn't caught up to that.

So I studied that handbook—over and over—and learned more about publicity, news writing and deadlines than many journalism majors whom I have since supervised.

For over ten years, I did volunteer publicity work for social and service organizations in California, Pennsylvania and Texas. I kept that PTA handbook at hand and, as it recommended, familiarized myself with deadlines and writing style of the media to which I submitted releases. I also learned parliamentary law and served as president of many clubs. I learned to set up photo opportunities which interested the newspaper and became well enough acquainted with the media people that many of them looked upon me as an unpaid staffer.

Now things were warming up to newspaper, but I didn't realize it.

In a tiny Texas town, my next-door neighbor was a journalism graduate who was the correspondent for the weekly newspaper in the county seat.

When she was on vacation, sick or having a baby, I filled in for her, but she received the twenty-five-cent-per-column-inch check. On December 29, 1957, I took correspondent copy to the newspaper office and reminded the editor that Doris would be back from vacation the next week. He twirled around to face me, motioned to a chair and said, "Have a seat. I want to talk to you." My only thought as I sat down was, "What have I done wrong?" Then came one of the biggest surprises of my life.

The editor wanted to hire me half-time as a writer for $35 a week. That was $1.75 an hour when minimum wage was way below that figure.

Remember, this was 1957. Though my husband had always been

supportive of my work, which after the Navy job included such activities as part-time hostess and appliance demonstrator in a furniture store, door-to-door sales of Christmas cards or small household appliances, I told the editor I would have to talk to my husband before I gave him an answer. As expected, my husband said: "Do it if you want to."

So on January 9, 1958, two days before my third daughter's third birthday, I reported for work, not knowing what I was really supposed to do but feeling confident that the editor would guide me. He did. But not for long.

He left for a better job. I got a new editor and his philosophy and mine on people coverage soon clashed. He was from deep East Texas where blacks were still treated with no respect, and I felt the newspaper was obliged to treat all persons equally and with dignity. For the only time in my career, I went over the editor's head and discussed the disagreement between the editor and myself with the publisher because that newspaper, in my five years of reading it, had not practiced the discriminatory policy the new editor espoused.

Thank goodness the publisher supported past policy. The editor became my friend and teacher. He was a wonderful yarn teller.

If you have ever worked at a weekly newspaper, you know you must learn about all departments, though one person may be the "department." I learned to take subscriptions, classified ads, roll single wraps, make up hot type pages, run the engraving machine, use a camera, supervise the darkroom technician, inventory and order photo supplies, cover all kinds of general assignment beats and write football (in Texas, that's very important!).

I had been a newspaper reader since I was very young, and when I arrived in Texas in 1953, I sampled several dailies until I found a really good one. It had good local writing, comprehensive wire service coverage and an editorial page where clearly reasoned editorials presented the paper's point of view. I also read the local weekly from cover to cover.

When I started doing general assignment work for the weekly, I began my own training manual. Each day I clipped samples of stories from the daily—particularly about types of events I had not covered—and pasted them in a notebook for reference.

My publisher and editor knew I had never taken a journalism course in my life, and they thought I was a really quick study on general assignment work. They didn't know about my self-help manual. Eighteen months later, I went to work full time as managing editor, with a new publisher carrying the title "Publisher and Editor." Our paper went to three times a week.

I soon figured out why I liked the job so much. I'd be a career student if I had the money, but I didn't. And general assignment work was just like going to school because I was learning everyday and meeting interesting people. The courthouse officials went out of their way to teach me what went on in their offices. They were flattered with the coverage because for years they had been woefully neglected. City hall and school personnel reacted in the same way.

One spring Thursday, we received three brand new twin lens reflex cameras and flashes. The publisher, our utility writer, the sports editor and I spent most of the morning reading instruction manuals and doing hands-on stuff with the cameras. About 12:45 we got a call about a new oil field coming in that morning at a little town twelve miles away. The publisher sent me off to cover the story with an untried camera and a mind void of oil field knowledge. But I did it. I really did it. There were no friendly officials to spoon-feed me information, no publicity-eager oil men to prime me with background and statistics. I talked to the rig superintendent, the driller, and some of the roughnecks and got the story, as well as good, printable photos. The only point in my favor was the well was on school district property and I didn't have to hassle over intruding on private property.

Succeeding on that assignment gave me confidence in my ability to gather information and was probably one of the most important events in my newspaper career. After a few months, the publisher had enough faith in me that he would leave town for a week or so with me in charge of the editorial department.

We weren't a timid small-town paper. We took stands on local issues and we printed all of the news—good and bad—regardless of who was involved. For the next two years, we won first places in news writing and news photography from the Texas Press Association, most of which was my work. And did I work! And did I love every minute of it! And was my world expanding! But it was too good to last.

The publisher, who was part owner, left and the absentee-owner group sent in a close-to-retirement circulation manager as publisher and a fresh-out-of-college kid as editor. The local editorials stopped. They discouraged, but did not forbid, coverage of controversial subjects or events. Staff morale was so low I could hardly keep them or myself producing.

The locals protested and within a year, the company sent in an experienced editor. We began to recover but were still allowed no local editorials without headquarters' approval and the new editor was not happy. Within a year, he left for the managing editor's position at the *Greenville Herald Banner,* a seven-morning paper. And I was breaking in another editor.

I wasn't happy, but I had to have a job so I kept giving my work the best possible effort. I had for several years been a correspondent for a metropolitan daily and was learning from the guidance of the state editor. That helped keep me busy.

Within six months, I had a call from my former editor, now in Greenville. He wanted me as courthouse reporter for the daily paper. I didn't know if I could do it but a friend, who had worked for daily papers, told me, "The only difference is that you clean out your notebook everyday and that is easier."

So on October 17, 1966, I reported to the *Herald Banner,* feeling much as I had on that day some seven years earlier when I went to cover the new oil field. And my friend was right. It was easier to clean out your notebook everyday. The satisfaction was greater in seeing daily stories as they developed, rather than constantly looking for updates or new leads to make three-day-old stories new for readers who were blanketed by dailies covering the same events.

In Greenville, I was immediately accepted by the staff and the courthouse officials who were surprised, chagrined and pleased with my knowledge of their work. The editor, the city hall reporter and I had regular morning meetings to plan the day's stories. My former editor, now the managing editor, worked nights and I didn't get to talk to him much. Within six months, the editor died and my friend became editor. The morning conferences continued and I was considered part of the editorial department management team, even though the city hall reporter had been made managing editor.

Before the year was out, the editor left for health reasons, the managing editor was promoted to editor and I was managing editor. That was a lot of change in less than two years, and I was supervising ten people instead of three.

This time, I didn't feel like I was going to a new oil field. This was where all my past experiences melded into the new skills I needed.

Organization was my first priority. I started a daily run sheet to keep track of the flow of pages from editorial to production. A futures book was set up to record needed advance and follow stories so coverage could be assigned. And other planning tools were developed to modernize and keep us operating in a rapidly changing news world.

It was a tumultuous time in our city and county, and we had lots to editorialize about. We were also stretched beyond staff capacity to cover our readership area. The *Herald Banner* was not only the single daily in our county but in two adjacent counties and parts of two other counties in which it circulated, though several small weeklies served the area outside of Greenville. We did not have the staff to do daily area coverage, so in December 1969, we hired our first area reporter.

Then in February 1970 the *Herald Banner's* parent company, Harte-Hanks of San Antonio, Texas, started an editorial training program for our smaller dailies. Greenville was selected as the training site and my education class training was called upon to help me teach real-life newspapering to the fifty or so trainees who have gone through the ten-week program in the last thirteen years.

Remember the mood of the country in the early seventies. The young were challenging the establishment and "new" journalism, with its advocacy positions, was invading the media. I did not object to innovations in news coverage, because there were new activities to be covered. But I did not agree with reporters being allowed to draw conclusions or make statements of editorial position in news stories.

So one Monday in August 1972, the publisher asked me into his office. He wanted to know if I would be in charge of the editorial department until a new editor arrived a month later. He was planning to replace the current editor. The next month was a real challenge to all the motivational and people-management skills I had acquired. Not one other person on the young staff had ever worked for any other editor and they were stunned by the turn of events. But by the end of the week, they were functioning again and were back to good, productive work when the new editor arrived.

My personal thoughts lingered on the fact that this would be the sixth editor in my career, and I was expected again to familiarize him with the newspaper, the community, the staff, the departmental planning and management and myriads of other pertinent local facts and figures. I thought about wanting the position of editor, though under the circumstances, this was not the time. Besides, a new editor had already been hired.

Why did I think I was qualified? It was not just my fourteen years of experience which could have been nonexpanding in skill and knowledge. It was the breadth, depth and scope of my experience in reporting, editorial writing, photography, copy editing, page layout and headline writing, assignment planning, staff management and general knowledge of the operation of all departments which must work together to produce a good newspaper. A small daily is not all that different from a weekly in the self-education opportunities available.

In addition, I had built upon the PTA manual by years of study of trade publications and review of as many newspapers—good and bad—as I could get my hands on. In 1968, I had become a member of the Texas Press Women, an affiliate of the National Federation of Press Women. I seriously attended all possible professional workshops, seminars and speeches at district, state and national meetings, especially those related to management skills and professional self-improvement. And I learned much through association with other professionals from across the state and nation. It was stimulating and educational to have such contacts through NFPW, as the male editors attended all the state press meetings and did not generally share knowledge with me when they returned.

So editor-number-six-to-be-broken-in firmly established my desire to be the editor.

As the previous ones had done, this new editor looked over my functions as managing editor and told me to continue in the same manner. About a year later, I learned he was marked for promotion to another paper and the *Herald Banner* was destined to have still another editor.

This time I let the publisher know I wanted the job and asked to be officially considered. He said he felt the editor needed to be a strong man. I agreed that the editor needed to be a strong person and reiterated my interest in the job.

I didn't get it. But I did direct the department for two months until the seventh-editor-to-break-in arrived. The staff immediately disliked and distrusted him. Two things made him the object of staff ridicule: First, he wrote an editorial endorsing an Arkansas candidate for governor; and second, a national newspaper magazine carried an article about his Arkansas successor who had been selected to "replace an inept editor."

The best I could do was manage around him and try—not very successfully—to keep up staff morale and productivity.

He lost all final vestiges of respect when he wrote and published an editorial which the city hall reporter had told him was erroneous. And when city hall descended upon him en masse, he put the blame on the reporter. Several weeks before he was fired, the publisher told me what was coming and said he intended to make me editor.

That didn't quite materialize. The publisher took the title of publisher and editor and made me executive managing editor with full charge of the department but with no budgetary responsibility. This was in the spring of

1975 with the budget for the year already set, but I had not been included in its planning and knew none of its details. Therefore, I had to go to the publisher or business manager every time I needed to spend money to find out if I had such funds budgeted. That soon became an inconvenience for them so I started to receive the monthly report for editorial and in the fall was given the planning guidelines for the coming year's budget proposal.

In the spring of '77, I was officially named editor. The only reason the publisher gave was that he was tired of taking all those telephone calls that should be coming to me. He was a man who gave out few back pats but you came to know he was pleased with the department's operation as long as he did not hand out brickbats.

That publisher—a man with a lifelong newspaper background—retired at the end of 1981 and we started with a new publisher who was twenty-five years younger, had a business management background and some six years of newspaper experience.

The transition was smooth and my sex was apparently no barrier to his acceptance of my responsibility and competence.

For example, when we were notified of the timetable for installation of our electronic editing system, I was assigned to draw up the plans for editorial remodeling to accommodate wiring, placement and accessibility of work stations, with no question of my ability to do so.

After twenty-five years in newspapering, the last six as editor of a 13,000-circulation, seven-day morning publication, I find I was one of the early women editors and hope my performance was a factor in the appointment of more women in my company and others.

Sex was never a handicap in general assignment work. The challenge was convincing those I was writing about that I had the intellectual capability to understand and relate their stories.

An unbridled curiosity throughout my life that led me to ask questions, read widely and dare to attempt the unknown has been my strongest asset. As the oldest daughter in a sonless family, I was expected to be an achiever and my parents never told me my mind was limited by gender.

Sex was a handicap in becoming a department head because the old "bogie story" about men not being willing to take instructions from women was alive and well. But with the publisher's faith and support, we proved that men and women are mainly influenced by the knowledge, skill and managerial ability of a supervisor, who is aware of their professional strengths and weaknesses and who is available to advise and guide as they need.

The publisher was not sure of community acceptance when he named me editor, but there was no problem. Perhaps my 10½ years in Greenville as a very visible and frequently by-lined general assignment writer who had covered many controversial, long-running stories without bias or prejudice was responsible, coupled with community acceptance of the judgment of the publisher.

Participatory decision making is my basic style of mangement. Creative writers need someone with whom to discuss their ideas and problems; someone who will look at how a situation fits in with the overall picture or perhaps distorts it; someone who will not fence in their minds with taboos and sacred cows; and someone who will encourage and assist them to finding a way to tell a story that needs to be told.

Participatory decision making, in my opinion, does not diminish authority but increases it because all involved are committed to the decision they have helped reach.

Because most of our replacement personnel are fresh out of school or have limited experience, on-going training is mandatory and it is a never-ending pleasure for me to observe their progress and development. They all know that the better they achieve individually, the better the department as a whole performs.

We are a team with backup players and substitutes, so we are prepared to handle any situation. We have no prima donnas, though we do have first-rate starters in each area of expertise and they are generous in sharing with and teaching other staff members.

Learning how to interview and hire the best possible replacements is one of the most important skills for an editor. Trial and error have taught me not to hire the first body that walks in the door and not to hire someone's friend just because that person wants a job. The good staff we have deserve good colleagues who can carry their own load and readily contribute.

Teaching every staff member a wide variety of tasks and beats is essential, particularly at a small newspaper. An editor's performance is strengthened and enhanced by a well-trained, versatile staff which can produce a good product with or without the editor's presence. Confidence in their performance is probably the best morale builder any editor can provide the staff.

To other women who would be editors, my best advice is to learn general managerial and financial skills, along with every detail possible about how the newspaper as a whole is produced and delivered. Never turn down a challenging assignment and never turn in a piece of work, no matter how trivial, on which you have not done the best possible job.

Learn to make decisions based on facts and logic, and learn to understand the gamesmanship language used by many males to support the team concept of working together, as well as learning how to be a real team member.

Do not expect any promotion to come your way just because you are female. Promotions, generally, are earned by those who continue to study, learn, welcome new challenges, grow in professional accomplishments and exhibit a sincere dedication to the profession.

I got into newspapering through the back door. I now proudly walk out the front door every evening with the satisfaction of serving our readers and our community.

That's a great feeling.

But I haven't forgotten the awe and exhilaration of covering that "new oil field" some twenty-three years ago.

Dennis Floss

DONNA HAGEMANN

Dennis Floss

DONNA HAGEMANN

Donna Hagemann

DONNA HAGEMANN, 30, is executive editor of the *Daily Press* and the
Observer-Dispatch, Gannett-owned dailies in Utica, New York.

She is a native of New Jersey, and a 1973 high honors graduate of
Syracuse University.

Hagemann began working for newspapers when she was seventeen,
holding a variety of jobs with weeklies in central Jersey. After graduating
from college, she joined the *Courier-News,* a Gannett daily in
Bridgewater, New Jersey. She was a reporter for three and a half years. In
1977, she was named assistant night editor; in 1978, assistant city editor; in
1979, assistant managing editor/metro; and in 1980, assistant managing
editor. She transferred to Utica as the top editor in February 1981.

Hagemann attended the American Press Institute, and has returned
twice as a guest lecturer. She has done extensive public speaking.

She is a member of the American Society of Newspaper Editors, the
New York State Society of Newspaper Editors, the Society of Professional
Journalists and Women In Communications, Inc. She serves on the boards
of directors of the Mohawk Executive Forum and the Syracuse University
Alumni Association, and works with her church's youth organization.

Hagemann is cited in *Who's Who of American Women.* She was named
an Outstanding Young Woman of America in 1982, and a Young Career
Woman by the New York Federation of Business and Professional Women
in 1981.

She and her husband, Jerome Donovan, live in Whitesboro, New York.

The closer you get to the top, the more difficult it becomes.

Or rather, the more aware you become of how very difficult it is.

Perhaps one reason so many of us have continued to push, and to strive
for better positions, and battled for due recognition, is that we didn't
realize just what we were getting ourselves into. It's not the difficulty of
doing the job that's such a challenge; we're all very capable of handling
very difficult tasks. It's all the peripheral things that seem to sprout up
when you're in top management—and you're a woman.

I've always wanted to be in "newspaper management." Even when I
was a teenager eagerly typing classified ad copy, or revising address labels
for weeklies in central New Jersey, I always knew that someday I wanted
to run a newspaper. I also knew that the route I would take would be

through the news end—after all, I reasoned, news is what newspapers are all about. But I realized that there are other very important (nay, crucial) parts of newspapering that go beyond the typewriter—the business and production ends, for example—and that, they, too, would have to become part of a repertoire of understanding.

And so I got my feet wet by doing a little here and a little there, but always watching carefully the person in charge of what was going on here or there.

And then came the "big break"—not the move into management, but the move into a real, live daily newspaper, the *Courier-News,* a Gannett-owned daily (circulation 60,000) in central New Jersey.

It was the summer between my junior and senior years in college, and I was one of a cluster of young, eager, and mostly female student interns. For me, the breaks broke right: The religion editor took a few months off and dubbed me her replacement, giving me an opportunity to spend an entire summer handling my "own" weekly page of features, news and bulletin board items. Other editors seemed especially open to assigning a myriad of articles, despite my inexperience. And I worked for an editor/publisher who taught me the right things at the right time.

That man, John Curley, now editor of Gannett's *USA TODAY,* has continued to hold a very strong influence on my development as a newspaperperson. He worked with me from the very beginning to tighten and brighten my writing, snazz up my layouts and show me that cute headlines don't necessarily tell the story.

When he left the *Courier-News* three months after I joined the paper as a full-time staffer, I remember feeling as if the Great Guru who had guided my life was abandoning me. But he continued to encourage me, and challenge me, from his other assignments. Over the years, he's helped me reach some of the most difficult decisions I've faced: whether to leave the city desk and move into corporate publications (I stayed); whether to leave Gannett—and a good shot at a management position—to accept an excellent (but lower) title with another newspaper group (again I stayed); and whether to leave the paper where I'd grown up, and learned my way, to tackle running a couple of newspapers on my own (I went).

As they were made, they were all crucial, soul-wrenching decisions. They would, I knew, shape my professional development for many years to come. For example, a shift to corporate communications would have opened up a whole avenue of opportunities, but outside of daily newspapers. Or a move to a busy city desk on an aggressive, classy metro daily would have helped my editing and news talents, but perhaps hold me back from learning about top management.

Each of those decisions was reached after a lot of thought as to what I wanted to do now, what I most enjoyed doing now, and how that could help me do what I wanted to later on. The most important factor, however, was the priority "now." I feel that there are so many opportunities in communications that other experiences could be tried later on. But what I wanted "now" was to learn *how* to manage a newspaper, and to do it.

The crises I face now as an executive editor of a morning, evening and Sunday operation, are quite different from those challenges I faced when I first walked through the door of the *Courier-News*. The early problems were typically those of a green, perhaps too-eager young reporter: an overwhelming desire to please (which sometimes got in the way of asking the tough questions); embarrassing naivete, and some colleagues who did not welcome my enthusiasm and ambition.

I will confess to still wanting to please, but now that may be the very reason why I ask the tough question. I also will admit to still being naive. And I still encounter colleagues who do not welcome my enthusiasm and ambition. But those problems are manifested in very different ways for an editor than they were for a reporter. And I think they're more threatening and frightening now than they were at the other end of the organization chart.

My path was speedy, but followed rather typical patterns: beat reporter to bureau reporter to copy editing to city desk to assistant managing editor. Along the way I found that the things they taught me in journalism school—how to write a lead, how to put together a page, how to liven up a headline—started to give way to a need to know some things they never talk about during those four years—how to quiet a staff rebellion, how to negotiate with a Guild, how to deal with a staffer whose ex-wife has kidnapped his children and whose girlfriend has just been killed by her estranged husband.

The challenges of managing are enormous. There are so many people whose lives you can directly affect. And the decisions you make have a much greater impact at this level. They affect an entire staff, sometimes an entire building, and usually your entire readership. And the criticism, or Monday-morning quarterbacking from your fondest critics.

I had never really believed that being a woman made a difference. I had been raised with the idea that you can do anything you set your mind to. And who cares what your sex is. So it came as a rather unpleasant surprise to realize that there are indeed people out there who do care, and that they can make life very difficult because they care and they'd like to do something about it.

As I said before, the closer you get to the top, the more difficult it becomes. Female reporters are threatening, some people say, but not nearly so threatening as female editors. After all, there are many young women out there working as writers and reporters. They can easily be melded into the general fray of reporters. But there are not a whole lot of female editors. So they tend to stand out from the crowd.

In Utica, I felt this whole "problem" of being female particularly acutely. Utica, in the middle of Upstate New York, is an absolutely delightful place to live. It's safe, clean, the people are extremely friendly, and there is a lot to do—restaurants, theater, shopping, the great outdoors.

Utica is also, historically, a very ethnic, blue-collar town. Of course, the demographics are changing; the population is becoming younger, better educated, higher paid.

But there is still that core of old customs and traditions that endures.

As a Gannett import to the top editor's position here, I naturally aroused curiosity and skepticism. First, I was a woman (and that really does matter); then I was young—twenty-eight when named to the job, and looking maybe twenty-five. I also was an outsider—someone not born, bred and educated on Utica-area soil. And I was replacing (not succeeding, replacing) a man who had been with the Utica newspapers for forty years.

That's a lot of baggage to bring to a new job.

At first, it didn't matter. I was too busy even to notice. And I was too excited with the prospect of working with two newspapers and having two opportunities to try new ideas and launch new projects.

The stress, especially in the beginning, was tremendous. I had not only moved away from the community where I had lived my entire life, but I had done it alone, was trying to do it in a very visible position, and buying a house (my first) all at the same time. My body reacted in a very understandable way: It rebelled. And so as I prepared to address a local gathering of 300 senior citizens, I found myself instead collapsing and then spending twenty-four hours in a hospital until they could figure out what was wrong.

The problem was not terribly severe—hypoglycemia, probably brought on by stress and hotel living. A strict diet and warnings to calm down were the doctor's orders.

Maybe that experience alerted me to some things I should have learned earlier but still don't quite follow: Don't bite off more than you can chew; don't try to prove yourself to everyone right away; let some things take their course and don't try to build Rome (or rebuild Utica) in a day.

Over the intervening couple of years, I've learned some other things: Being a woman does matter. You get treated differently—especially at first when people are trying to get a reading on you. You're subject to much closer scrutiny and much sharper criticism from new colleagues, new readers, new bosses.

People still are threatened by women. By ambitious women. And particularly by bright women. The same qualities that "sold" you to the person who hired you often end up being the things that bother him or her the most—because they're the qualities of talent, and drive, and ability that make you a possible contender for that person's job.

The experience becomes more pronounced the closer you get to the top because it's more concentrated. You're no longer one of five summer interns, or one of four city editors among dozens of editors. You're one or two of a few, and that makes you stand out more. You've been able to work your way through the crowd and achieve some specialness. And that makes you threatening.

What can help is continuing to remind yourself how much you enjoy your job and continuing to have fun doing it. It helps to know that there is so very much to do—and so very many different ways to do it—that when you start getting bored with one assignment, there's always another ready to be tried.

What can hurt—at least inside—is trying to put up with the hostility and the never-ending challenges to your position while you're trying to do your job. It can hurt to realize that doing your job the best you are able often isn't enough. And that being good sometimes isn't enough.

Those peripheral concerns—of politics, of having to make other people look good, of backing down in one battle because you're trying to save your energy for another—are faced by most people in top positions, not just women.

And just because there are those concerns does not mean they're not worth facing. There is a tremendous amount of personal development to be experienced by learning how to deal with the politics, and daily battles, and stepping aside to let someone else be in the limelight.

As trite as it sounds, every experience, no matter how bad it seems at the time, does help you grow and mature. And while it may not change the way you do things the next time around, it at least prepares you to be willing to accept the consequences.

Newspapering is a marvelous business. Few people have such an opportunity to help shape public opinion and to help shape progress. Of course, anyone wanting to have that power has to be willing to accept the criticism foisted by those people who don't share her way of thinking. Both internally—staff members and colleagues—and externally—the reader.

There is a visibility attached to being an editor that can be unnerving. The feeling that you can't head to the hardware store in an old Ohio State stained and holey T-shirt for more paint remover because you just might run into a local council member who wants to discuss the pending sales tax.

The feeling that you have to be "out and about" sharing in events in your community. Because, after all, you're setting your newspaper up as a reflection of the community, and how can you reflect what you don't experience?

That visibility can intrude on your personal life. And, again, the closer you get to the top, the less private your personal life seems. If you're single, every development in your social life is observed, analyzed and commented. If you're married, your whole family becomes public property, subject to scrutiny. And if you're in the process of changing marital status—from single to married, or vice versa—you seem to become fair game for virtually everyone's opinion.

That has been very difficult for me to accept. I want to scream that I have a life quite separate and apart from the newspaper, and that I'd like to conduct it on my own, thank you. But I realize that as editor in what has been called "the biggest small town in America," I must be willing to undergo this scrutiny and to share more of my privacy than I would like.

There have been many very difficult professional decisions I've faced in the past nine years: job changes, potential career changes, transfers. But the most difficult ones are yet to come.

When, for example, will the intrusion on my private and personal life become so annoying that the sheer ecstacy of running a newsroom no longer balances it out?

When will the internal drive to go higher, and higher, and higher finally say enough; I like where I am.

What will the people who have played such an important role in forming my professional life say when, or if, such a decision is made? Will they agree that enough is OK, or will they want more?

Will we women who've always thought we could have it all—career, husband, family—begin to reconsider and decide that maybe two out of three isn't so bad after all?

How will those of us who decide to opt for the latter two handle no longer being in power, no longer bringing home a comfortable paycheck, no longer being in the limelight?

Each year I tell myself that the next few years will be the most important of my life; that they will hand me the most difficult decisions I've ever made. And each year I say, whew, that wasn't so bad; what's next?

What's next is to continue to appraise where I am, and what I'm doing, and how and where I'm doing it. I cannot conceive of having a job that is more fun than editing a newspaper. I cannot conceive of a job that provides more opportunity to make yourself heard and felt. And I cannot conceive of a job that provides more instant satisfaction.

But, then again, five years ago I never would have conceived of myself living and working and being married in Utica, New York.

And so I'm keeping myself tuned to this same station, which has been pretty good in rewarding the hard work and difficult decisions of a near decade. And I'm leaving myself open to a whole world of opportunities. And I'm hoping those people who helped along the way—the demanding city editor, the compatriot assistant editors, the gifted writers, the Great Guru of years past—will continue to help. And, most important, I will try to understand whatever new paths I choose to follow.

Judith Olausen

BEVERLY KEES

Vickie Kettlewell

BEVERLY KEES

Beverly Kees

BEVERLY KEES is executive editor of the *Grand Forks,* North Dakota, *Herald.* She supervises news and editorial operation of the seven-mornings-a-week newspaper serving fourteen counties in North Dakota and Minnesota (circulation 35,000). She previously held a variety of positions at both the *Minneapolis Star* and the *Tribune,* including assistant managing editor of the *Tribune.*

She is a graduate of the University of Minnesota where she was editor of the campus daily.

Ms. Kees has taught beginning journalism at the College of St. Thomas and is the author of three cookbooks.

In Grand Forks, she is a member of the board of the symphony, the Red Cross chapter and the public radio station.

What comforts me most after several years in newsrooms is the knowledge that one can screw up from time to time and still live to see the dawn.

There are a number of helpful books out now for working women that would have spared me some learn-by-doing grief had they been around during my professional infancy. Reading "10 Dumb Things to Avoid for a Successful Career," I realize I did nine of them.

(I missed the tenth. I never got pregnant by a boss, partly because even on my dumbest days I knew that was not the way to get a promotion; partly because none of my bosses ever asked me.)

Part of the advice is to have a clear idea of where you want to go and to develop a plan for getting there. I always knew from childhood where I wanted to go, but the goal changed from year to year—actress, opera singer, nurse and English teacher. The teaching goal coincided with my senior year in high school, so I enrolled at the University of Minnesota.

I had been editor of my high school paper largely because my father had been editor of his and it seemed like a nice family tradition. It was more fun working on the paper than in English class, but it didn't strike me as a serious career. ("A hard life for a woman," my mother told me.)

As I prepared to set off for freshman week on campus, a friend told me to stop by the *Minnesota Daily* office during the paper's welcoming coffee hour because the editor, a neighbor of hers, was a good-looking bachelor.

He was a good-looking bachelor. He was also engaged to the news editor. But the *Daily* looked like fun and they were nearly shanghaiing bodies off the street to be reporters, so I signed up for the staff.

Over the next four years, I changed from an English major-journalism minor to an English-journalism double major to a journalism major-English minor, driving my adviser to a sabbatical my junior year. English instructors wrote "too breezy, too journalese" on my themes, which I took as a clue.

In the olden days, the Minneapolis Star and Tribune Company had a lunch on Lincoln's Birthday for a dozen graduating seniors, half in news, half in advertising. As editor of the *Daily* by that time, I got one of the invitations.

My mother told me I should wear a hat because that's what proper ladies did when going to meet potential employers. Typical of the age, I responded, "Motherrrrrrr." I wore the hat, a half-circle of small white feathers that clung to my head, I hoped unnoticed. Of course, I was the only one wearing a hat.

At the luncheon, we seniors were scattered around the table, intermingled with newspaper executives. Following the meal, we were each allowed to ask the execs a question about the place. The questions were fine. "Following the strike of 1962, what were the ramifications regarding. . . ." "What is your philosophy of journalism on the matter of. . . ."

When it was my turn, I asked: "Will you have any jobs in June?"

There was a hush, then a nervous titter. The publisher muttered something about the table of organization being full up and the questioning moved on. After lunch each of us received an application form to fill out and send in if we were interested. I sent mine in and was the only one of the group to be hired in the newsroom. I could see them going through the applications, coming to mine and saying, "Oh, yes, the lippy one in the hat."

My first job was in the old women's department. I covered women's political and education groups as well as doing such traditional features as "Woman Behind the Man." It taught me a lot. We had to wrestle interesting features out of pretty thin gruel some days which is a lot tougher than covering a fire or a city council meeting where the news is obvious and relatively easy to get.

After three years of this, my request for a transfer to the city desk was granted and I became a suburban reporter, where most male reporters started out. "A sink or swim situation, but there's no reason you can't handle it," one of the male editors said. The job was, in fact, considerably easier than the women's department as other feature section writers over the years would discover.

After a year of dog leashing laws and zoning and planning commission meetings, I began to get restless again. Listening to me grouse one evening was the *Star's* night editor, William R. Greer, who had taught me a while back to use a sizing wheel to size photos. It wasn't a part of my job, but it seemed a useful thing to know. Greer said he had tried to teach that to other staff members, some of whom flatly refused because they were afraid they would be called upon to do that work if word got out they could. Greer was of the school that taught one to learn everything one could about everything one could because one never knew when it might come in handy. Greer was a good teacher.

He suggested that if I didn't like the stories I was doing, I should come up with a dozen ideas for better stories. Editors are always looking for good story ideas, he said.

I could take some positive action to solve my own problem? I reeled from the impact of this startling concept. (Women in those days were taught to keep their noses to the grindstone, their backs straight, their hands folded and their knees together and wait for someone to come along to solve their problems. Which is why we had so many problems.)

I dreamed up a dozen story ideas and submitted them, the editors picked out a few for me to work on and life brightened. A couple of the stories were business oriented. My business background was Economics I and II—guns and butter charts that left me glassy-eyed and off the honors lists at the university. Economics in real life was a lot more interesting.

Emboldened by my first attempt at taking action, I submitted to the city desk a resume for a job as a business writer. Laugh! You could have heard them all over the metropolitan area. Word must have gotten out about my Econ I and II grades.

Shortly after, I left for a vacation in Canada. While I was gone, a business reporter resigned. When I returned, I had his job. For two years I covered real estate and construction and the odd business story that didn't fit into the beats of the senior business reporters. I loved every minute of it and soon knew more about concrete than anyone on my block.

I submitted a plan for a real estate and construction section about the time the paper was planning to launch a food section. The editors must have figured, "She wants a section, let's give her this one," because they never bothered to ask if I could cook before offering me the job as food section editor.

Happily, one of the editors took me aside before the offer was made to tell me about it, anticipating my response. Food section! After all those years of fighting to get out of the old women's department! Food section? There went my dream of Beverly Kees in a trench coat covering World War III.

The editor told me to give it some thought. It was a chance to be supervisor and to plan the evening paper's first regular special section. (The *Tribune,* our morning sister down the hall, had special sections on Sunday.) Also, the job wouldn't be forever.

By the time the formal meeting with the editors occurred, I had given the idea thought and decided to accept. Everybody eats. Surely there was a way to make a food section appealing to a broad readership.

The new section, Taste, was launched October 1, 1969, and for the next four years gave me some of my warmest moments in the newspaper business. Because here were no precedents to follow, we could experiment and produced useful food stories along with light features on the tongue and music to play to create certain moods while dining. ("Stars and Stripes Forever" to get folks moving apace through a buffet line. The effects of romantic music are trickier to pinpoint; it could get one either a proposal or a proposition with the dessert course.)

Men and women, Republicans and Democrats, dieters and overeaters could all enjoy the food section. No one ever accused us of slanting a recipe. One woman told us she and her husband went to bed with the Taste section every Wednesday night. Taste was a way to pack readers' names into the paper through recipe exchanges and contests and a restaurant recipe request column. Unlike the front page that had to respond to whatever was going on that day, the food section was created from our own imaginations and intuition. We had a better opportunity than in any other part of the paper to listen to readers and respond to their requests. It was a good experience and got me closer to our readers than concrete or sewer assessment hearings ever could.

After the first couple years on Taste, I got my job down to forty hours a week and my bosses apparently figured I was slipping away from them. They named me editor of special sections so I could supervise Taste and the daily Variety section.

Then I got a call from the publisher, the late Robert W. Smith, who asked casually if I would be interested in an idea of his—a lateral movement training program in which people would be transferred out of their regular departments to work in other departments of the paper for nine months to a year. Would I be interested?

Frankly, I was appalled. The newsroom was the only place that interested me and it was where I wanted to spend my life. But I wasn't a complete ninny. When one's publisher asks, "What do you think of my new idea?" one does not give him the raspberry and fly from the room. And so I wound up the guinea pig in the Minneapolis Star and Tribune Company's lateral movement program.

For nine months I worked in the research planning department, a small group who worked for the publisher and did whatever research he needed to make decisions. If he wanted to start a new section or change ad rates or alter the circulation patterns, this department studied the matter and made proposals. It was a valuable experience and taught me more about how the rest of the building operated than all I had learned in the previous ten years.

It also paved the way for a new job. I spent the next six months as assistant to the editor of the *Tribune,* Charles W. Bailey, then became the company's first female assistant managing editor. Eventually in that job, I put together the newsroom's multimillion-dollar budget, processed job applicants, developed and supervised a couple of weekly feature sections, supervised a weekly Perspective (news feature) page, handled the newsroom's daily newshole requests to ad makeup, represented the newsroom at the weekly interdepartmental on-time committee, and did assorted other chores such as working on a committee to develop a staff job review system.

When I was learning a lot of these new duties, Frank Wright returned from the *Tribune's* Washington bureau to become managing editor and my new boss. At the same time we were getting our first video display terminals installed, reorganizing the staff, setting up new sections and hiring a lot of new people.

Wright and I were both putting in long days and the work load became oppressive. Wright kept dropping off more and more work and I got increasingly steamed. One day he sent over a letter from a French student asking to spend several months with us. "Handle this, please," Wright wrote across the top. That was it. In letters of flame, I wrote a memo saying I would be happy to handle his correspondence as well as my own if I weren't already on my knees from overwork, etc. Wright walked into my office carrying the smoking memo and said, "Don't get excited."

Behind clenched teeth, I said icily, "I'm not getting excited but I'm not going to do it."

You know what he said? "OK."

Wright hadn't known I was overworked because I hadn't told him. I nearly bit the man's head off because he hadn't read my mind! To his everlasting credit, Wright did not pitch me headfirst out the door but helped ease my workload.

It was a valuable lesson but one I have to keep relearning. Often, when I have a problem, I discover it is because I haven't clearly explained what the problem is to the person who can solve it but, rather, expected someone to read my mind, to know intuitively what should be done. That is real dumb.

Another important lesson of those years was learning the need for contacts. An informal management women's group was set up at the Star and Tribune Company. We met for lunch in the building every other week, sometimes to hear a speaker or to discuss a particular subject, sometimes just to meet and talk. There were several women in supervisory jobs around the building, but not many in any department and many of us had never met. This group provided us with conduits to other departments and, as we moved on, to other newspapers. We had new places to go to get questions answered and to find help and occasionally solace. We could share problems and test out ideas. It gave us the camaraderie men knew on the softball field or racquetball court. It was enormously helpful.

Meanwhile, back in the newsroom, I got restless again after a few years and started asking the company bosses about the possibilities of being a managing editor someday. I was told I wasn't qualified because I hadn't worked on the news desk. I pointed out that neither had the current editor or managing editor.

Bailey had long been a supporter of promoting women and I figured he would be candid. He was also planning to go back to writing after ten years as editor so he would not be making the decision about my future.

What management skills could I learn on the news desk that I hadn't already learned or couldn't learn in the job I had? Bailey admitted there weren't any, but there was a perception I needed the experience because I hadn't moved up in the traditional male route—political reporter, city editor, news editor or Washington bureau. The conversation helped me see not what was fair or what ought to be, but what was. It was an eyeopener.

I was also beginning to read some of the those very helpful books coming onto the market, such as *The Managerial Woman* and *Games Mother Never Taught You*. I looked around the *Star* and *Tribune* and realized there was not one woman in a position of real authority in any line department (news, advertising, circulation, production) in the company. It was a shock.

This had been my home for eighteen years and I loved it. I liked and respected the people I worked for and felt my colleagues were like a second family. It was warm and comfortable. It also began to dawn on me my job was going nowhere. There would always be some job I hadn't done yet and I wasn't willing to start out all over again as a political reporter to prove I was a capable manager.

With sound, rational, intelligent reasoning, I decided to spend the first six months of 1981 deciding whether I should stay or go. I would talk to a lot of people, acquire information, study the matter, reach a decision based on facts and solid interpretation, and then form a plan. I knew the dismal statistics about the numbers of newspaper management jobs held by women and figured it would be a long, tough search if I decided to seek my fortune elsewhere.

On a Monday in February, I talked to a friend on the *Star* and told him what I planned to do in the coming months. The next day, Tuesday, I talked to a friend on the *St. Paul Pioneer Press* and told her the same thing. On Wednesday of that week, the then-publisher of the *Grand Forks* (North Dakota) *Herald*, Tom Schumaker, happened to call both my friend on the *Star* and my friend on the *Pioneer Press* and told them he was looking for a woman to hire for the Knight-Ridder paper. Did they have any names? Both gave him my name.

He called and asked me to come to Grand Forks for an interview. It was much too soon to be setting up interviews because I hadn't decided whether I was leaving the *Tribune* yet, and besides, Grand Forks was NORTH and I had always hated winter. If, after a lifetime, I was finally going to leave Minneapolis, I sure as heck was not going to move north. If I did move, the logical step was to a managing editor job on a large daily, not the executive editor job on a much smaller daily.

However, I hadn't been on a job interview in eighteen years, so I decided to meet with Schumaker to get in a little practice. Three months later I moved to Grand Forks, amid a lot of North Dakota weather jokes from my *Star* and *Tribune* friends.

Minneapolis then had one of its worst winters in history with record-setting snowfalls while Grand Forks was a comparative island of calm. The Star and Tribune Company went through great turmoil as the *Star* folded and a lot of people were laid off. I felt very lucky to be in Grand Forks.

The job gives me all the opportunities I need to learn to be a good editor. I'm not as good at the job as I plan to be, but I'm better than when I arrived.

I have figured out that the luck that got me various jobs over the years was invariably prompted by my own actions. If I hadn't asked for the business writer's job on the *Star,* no one would have thought of me when a business writer resigned. If I hadn't suggested a new section, no one would have thought of me when a new section was planned. If I hadn't talked to friends about looking for a job outside of Minneapolis, they would not have given my name to the publisher looking for a new executive editor.

A clear lesson that should be burned in my brain. It's not. I learn it over and over again as I sit around fretting about problems that get solved only when I take some positive action to solve them.

Another lesson: Nobody does it alone. Schumaker did not call me because he could see my brilliance shining 300 miles away. He called because my friends gave him my name. I would be thrilled if I could help them out the same way someday. If not them, then, in their names, someone else who needs a hand.

There is no question that women face some barriers that men do not, but it's not the barriers alone that hold us back. It is our belief that they will. As one who enjoys an occasional wallow in self-pity, I know how much easier it is to sit back and grumble rather than go after what I want. The latter requires an energy level I don't always have.

Several years ago, I interviewed Helen Gurley Brown. She said that after her book, *Sex and the Single Girl,* became a best seller, an acquaintance told her with a sniff, "I could have written that book." Brown replied, "Yes, but I did."

I remind me of that.

SUSAN H. MILLER

Brian Johnson

SUSAN H. MILLER

Brian Johnson

Susan H. Miller

SUSAN H. MILLER is executive editor of the *News-Gazette,* a 50,000-circulation A.M.-P.M. daily serving Champaign, Urbana, the University of Illinois and surrounding communities. She is responsible for the day-to-day operation of the newsroom through seventeen editions a week (one morning and two afternoon editions on weekdays, one edition Saturdays and Sundays), and also for *Illini Times,* a 15,000-circulation free weekly newsmagazine published by the *News-Gazette* for University of Illinois students. She has a staff of fifty persons. She hires and supervises, administers the budget, selects syndicated features and writes some editorials. She reports to the editor and general manager. Mrs. Miller holds a bachelor's degree from Stanford University, a master's from the Graduate School of Journalism at Columbia University in New York City, and a Ph.D. in communication from Stanford. She has worked for the *Bremerton,* Washington, *Sun,* the *Peninsula Times Tribune* in Palo Alto, California, and as a public information officer for school districts in Palo Alto and Montgomery County, Maryland.

Her husband, Bud, is a partner in a consulting firm in California. He travels to Illinois roughly once a month. They have no children.

My current job probably sounds like an ideal situation: executive editor of a 50,000-circulation A.M.-P.M. daily, in a university community, with an outstanding young, dedicated staff.

How did I get here? Through a combination of hard work, determination, good timing, good luck, a willingness to take chances and a long-standing love of journalism.

As did most women my age (I'm thirty-seven) and certainly most women of my background (I was born in a farming community in northern California), I grew up expecting to get married. Unlike most of them, I also wanted to be something else: I wanted to be a journalist.

My understanding of journalism has changed greatly over the years, and it wasn't until I was most of the way through a doctorate at Stanford that I became interested in newspaper management. But from the time I was sixteen, I wanted to be a journalist.

I fell into journalism because I liked to write. At one point I announced I wanted to be a poet, and my mother very firmly told me that nobody made any money being a poet. I wasn't raised to think in terms of a career, but I was raised to think in terms of working. My parents are both extremely practical, hard-working, self-made people. My father was a teacher and school administrator. My mother worked as a telephone operator. They were strict, and they had high ambitions for both children (I have an older brother).

When I was sixteen, I attended a conference for high school yearbook staffs, and one of the speakers suggested that we consider careers in journalism. I got a part-time job at my local paper, covering teen-age news, and worked summers at another paper for the next two years.

My choice of a journalism career was responsible for my selecting Stanford. At that time Stanford had one of the few accredited journalism programs in California. I honestly didn't understand how competitive admission to Stanford was, nor did I understand that my next move in schooling would greatly increase the difficulty of getting admitted. I went to the local community college for two years. At that time Stanford took far fewer undergraduate women than men, required all of them to live on campus, and had an attrition rate of just about zero. When I was accepted as a woman transfer student in 1964, I was one of a bare handful who were admitted that year.

In retrospect, going to Stanford was clearly a watershed move. Stanford ties would influence almost everything else I later did. Given the circumstances, I was just plain lucky it worked out.

I was there the last two years before the student unrest began. Stanford was still serene—an awesomely attractive collection of bright, ambitious people, living in a place and time when everything seemed possible. Robert Coles describes children in affluent families as growing up with a sense of "entitlement." That's exactly what it was like at Stanford.

I worked on the *Stanford Daily,* made mostly A's in my journalism classes, got pinned during winter quarter of my senior year. Allen "Bud" Miller had graduated from Princeton and was coaching the Stanford freshman crew team while he pursued a Ph.D. in electrical engineering. We met on a blind date on a camping trip to Yosemite and spent the first three months of our acquaintanceship stressing to each other that we were very independent people who had very definite plans for our lives that did not include any immediate plans for any serious relationships. We loved the song "Born Free." Pretty soon we spent all of our free time together. In the spring of my senior year I was named a *Mademoiselle* magazine guest editor, and left in May for a summer job in New York City, thinking I might stay in New York indefinitely.

I found *Mademoiselle* petty and trite; New York, dirty and rude. I spent nearly every weekend with Bud's family in Fairfield, Connecticut. At the end of the summer we were engaged. I moved back to Palo Alto, taking a public relations job at Stanford Hospital while he continued graduate school at Stanford. We were married the next June, and left for the East Coast and his next step in graduate school.

I got married because, after *Mademoiselle,* I didn't seriously consider any other options. Those days, everyone got married. Women, even bright, ambitious college-educated women, hadn't come to grips with the notion that a career is more than a series of jobs, and that one cannot have a career if one has no control over where one lives or for how long. The ideal seemed to be to work for a few years and then begin having a family.

It was taken on blind faith that either (1) one would not want to return to work after raising a family, or that (2) one would have absolutely no problem returning to work after raising a family. It seems incredible that women didn't bother to ask if there was any correlation between their expectations and the real world. All I know is that I didn't, nor did anyone I knew.

Bud had decided that electrical engineering was too confining. He'd always had an interest in government and public policy, and decided to take a master's degree in public affairs at the Woodrow Wilson School at Princeton. I found a reporting job at the local chain of weeklies. By mid-winter, working for a weekly was wearing thin. Two other reporters were applying to the Graduate School of Journalism at Columbia University in New York City. Bud had one more year to go at Princeton. Princeton was commuting distance (by train). I applied and was accepted.

But, in the process of deciding to apply, I had gone through a fundamental change in how I viewed my work, and Bud and I had articulated something that perhaps had surprised us both. It certainly surprised me.

I came home one day from work and announced that I wanted to go to Columbia, that I wanted a career in journalism, and that, unlike all of the other student wives we knew, I had no intention of quitting work to have a family when he finished school. Bud said that was fine. I explained it all again. (One had difficulty with graduate student husbands. They frequently did not pay attention.) Bud still said that was fine.

What neither of us had given much thought to when we decided to get married was how similar we were, and how different from other couples we knew. We both loved our work, and work was very important to our sense of self. Marriage had not changed that priority. While we enjoyed each other's company, we frequently spent long hours alone, immersed in work or studies. I liked the idea of being self-sufficient, intellectually and financially. Bud had no special desire to be the sole support of a family. Neither of us had the slightest desire to have children.

These latter points are matters couples nowadays probably discuss BEFORE they get married. I guess we were lucky that circumstances forced us to discuss them as early in our marriage as we did. We were even luckier that the conclusions we reached were compatible.

I find it easier to explain why I wanted a career than to explain why Bud is comfortable with a career-oriented wife. I think his attitude is partly the result of having a remarkable mother—brilliant, capable, good-natured—who, as the wife of a career Army officer, shouldered a lot of things single-handedly when Bud was growing up. I think it is partly the result of Bud's awesome self-confidence, which probably stems from being the kind of person who has always succeeded at everything he tried.

To the extent that some husbands are uncomfortable with their wives' success, there's often a deep-down insecurity about their own abilities. So far as I know, Bud has never viewed a career-oriented wife as anything other than an absolute asset. I've always felt he wanted a wife who could do everything, and do it well.

That's not to say that either of us fully understood the implications of a two-career marriage back then, or that we've got the perfect solution now. It's simply to say that we both possessed qualities that made such an arrangement possible.

So I became a student commuter for a year, getting up at 4:30 A.M. to catch the train into New York City, writing assignments in my head during the train ride home. I did some coursework in free-lance writing, and learned I had no temperament for that life. I have the discipline, but couldn't stand the uncertainty.

By temperament, I'm perfectly suited to the pace of a daily newspaper. I thrive on deadlines. I'm a pragmatist—comfortable with the realization that daily newspapering is the first rough draft of history. Searching indefinitely for the ultimate phrase is much less important to me than doing a decent story on deadline.

After my year at Columbia we moved back to Stanford, in line with Bud's plan to transfer to a new department and combine technical training and public policy work. The San Francisco Bay Area had just been hit by the journalism job crunch. Despite my master's degree, I couldn't get a reporting job. I took a post as a public information officer for the Palo Alto school district. The next year Bud did an internship in Washington, D.C. I got a similar job with the Montgomery County schools. Then we returned to Palo Alto. I went back to my Palo Alto job.

By now, it was becoming apparent to me that my resume was a shambles. Any potential newspaper employer would see a series of year-long PR jobs. I needed evidence that I did indeed take journalism seriously. I chose a most unusual route: I decided to get a Ph.D.

Heading the Ph.D. public affairs program in Stanford's Department of Communication was Bill Rivers, a former Washington correspondent and my undergraduate adviser. I knew he'd support my efforts to structure a program heavy on the practical aspects of print journalism. It took three years before I was accepted. (I finally enrolled in the local community college to take math courses to raise my GRE score.) It took me another three years to get a Ph.D.

In that time I worked like I've never worked before or since. I took classes in sociology and political science and anything I felt would give me a better grasp of the role of the media in modern society. I put a special emphasis on media criticism and performance. I did research and writing on media content and on treatment of women. In return for a fellowship that covered tuition, I taught beginning reporting—inventing the curriculum as I went along. And I finally understood, once and for all, why graduate student husbands sometimes don't pay attention when their wives talk to them.

For my dissertation, I spent three months in Washington, D.C., studying press coverage of Congress—looking at what gets covered, how those decisions are made, and the implications for Congress in terms of its own operation and public image.

In the process of interviewing Washington correspondents, I made a very interesting discovery: Many of these reporters, at the apex of the journalism pinnacle, had not terribly satisfying jobs. They were talented and hard-working, but they were literally at the mercy of their editors back home, who either weren't terribly interested in what they were writing or didn't have the space to run it. Veterans explained they could easily file three or four stories a day, but there was no point because, at best, one or two would be used.

So I decided that there was more to life than reporting. I decided to be an editor. A managing editor. Within five years.

The five years was somewhat arbitrary, but pragmatic. As with many careers, there is an age range ideal for certain positions. I'd lost roughly ten years with the combination of following my husband through graduate school, and getting my own Ph.D. When I finished my Ph.D. in 1976 I was thirty-one. I figured I needed to be a managing editor by thirty-six or thirty-seven.

I began sending out resumes. Newspapers in the Bay Area were intrigued by the Ph.D., but nobody offered me a job. One of the Stanford faculty members suggested a different plan: Pick a part of the country where you'd like to live and send a resume to every paper.

At that point, I faced a fundamental decision: Was I able to control where I lived? Was I bound to live where my husband did and make the best of the job market there? If I moved someplace else, was he bound to follow me? If not, what would happen to our marriage?

My husband was then working at SRI International and making plans with several friends to form a consulting company near Stanford.

I distinctly recall sitting on the couch in our apartment and telling my best friend, also a Ph.D. student in my department, that I simply couldn't just up and announce that I was moving somewhere else to take a job.

About two weeks later, I started sending resumes to Washington state.

I had simply run out of options.

There was no indication I was going to get a newspaper job anywhere within commuting range of the Bay Area. If I didn't find myself a job someplace, it would mean that all of the effort to go back for the Ph.D. would have been wasted. I briefly considered the option of taking a university teaching position. The market was excellent for women with some journalism experience and a Ph.D.

But I knew that wasn't what I wanted to do and that if I did, I'd never get back into newspapering. I don't know whether it was the three years I nearly killed myself getting the Ph.D., or the three years I struggled with math just so I could spend the next three years getting a Ph.D., or a sense of obligation to succeed at something because my department had taken so few women Ph.D. students. Whatever it was, I felt that this was my one big chance and that if I blew it, I wouldn't get another.

I agonized over my options with Bud. He sat with me night after night while I cranked out resumes and individually typed letters on the word processing equipment at SRI. I picked Washington state because he had a sister in Seattle. I drove up for a round of interviews and was offered a reporting job in Bremerton by an editor who was impressed with the Ph.D. He'd been in Stanford's first class of mid-career Professional Journalism Fellows.

Moving to Washington was akin to running away from home—or at least that's what everyone else thought. My friends and fellow Ph.D. students were appalled. Our respective families were dumbfounded. Most people, I think, assumed we had decided to get a divorce and just weren't letting on. Bud and I had decided there was no sense in his moving to Washington. He was in the midst of forming a new company, and everything we knew about one spouse following the other suggested that the follower ended up with a botched-up career.

We weren't sure how my job would work out. We weren't sure how his company would work out, but we were determined to give both a try. We decided to have what is now known as a commuter marriage—separate jobs in separate cities, getting together as often as possible.

That made sense to Bud and it made sense to me, until the barrage of negative reaction. I finally suggested, "You know, maybe this isn't such a good idea. Nobody thinks it's a good idea except you and me."

Bud simply asked, "Who else matters?"

We learned several things in going against the social grain. One is that it can generate tremendous amounts of hostility from people who either feel threatened that you are doing something different, or who perhaps are secretly envious that you had the courage to do something they didn't.

We counted our supporters on the fingers of one hand. We learned that pointing out that military couples have been living apart for years did quiet some people—but not many.

We also have had many conversations since then with other couples who are pondering a similar arrangement. All of them want to know the same thing: Is it OK? Can we do it? Our advice is always the same: It's OK if you think it's OK. Don't pay any attention to anyone else.

We've had two stints of commuter marriage—four years while I was working in Washington state, a year together, then another stint starting when I moved to Illinois in the summer of 1981. In some ways the first time was easier because we saw each other more often. (Bud was able to work out a schedule where he brought work up to our home in Washington and stayed about two weeks per month.) What helps this time is the knowledge that we've done it before and that it does work. When you finally get back together, you do still like your spouse. There are certain plusses. You make the time together count. You find tremendous pleasure in little things—like cooking dinner together or just talking. It is worth it if you both love your work. It is not the ideal way to live.

A commuter marriage is not glamorous. It is expensive (travel costs, two residences). It is lonely. It is a sacrifice I'm willing to make. Period.

When I started my reporting job in Bremerton I was covering the military (Puget Sound Naval Shipyard and the Trident submarine base ten miles to the north). I got the beat because (1) nobody else on the paper wanted it and (2) I figured that the military was the kingpin of the local economy, which made it the kingpin beat. I knew nothing about the military, but I learned. A year later I was named assistant city editor. For the next three years, in various combinations at various times, I handled the church page, entertainment section, lifestyle section and weekend magazine. I was editor for in-depth projects, wire editor, news editor on weekends.

My technique was simple: I'd figure out something that wasn't being done, or spot something that the person in charge had little interest in, and volunteer to take it on. That technique worked because I had the support not just of the editor, but especially of the managing editor. Everything that's been said about the importance of a mentor is true. He put me on the fast track. I can honestly say that everything I did, I did well, but there is no way I would have had those opportunities if he hadn't been willing actively to promote my career. I learned to supervise reporters, coordinate departments, brainstorm ideas, invent new sections. I got experience in hiring.

Ultimately, however, I'd gone as far as I could there. The top editors weren't about to be replaced and weren't about to retire. I interviewed for several months, and finally took a job as assistant city editor in Palo Alto, California, where the paper had recently been bought and was undergoing a massive change in staff and a redesign. I was attracted to the idea of (1) living in Palo Alto with my husband and (2) getting in on the ground floor of staffing changes that could enhance my career. It was a chancy move. The position I was taking—assistant city editor—was actually a step down from my post as newsfeatures editor, although at a somewhat larger paper (60,000 versus 35,000).

It turned out to be a disaster. Although I was given responsibility for supervising the in-depth reporting projects, I was one of several assistant city editors. The others were responsible for local coverage of specific geographic areas and had first call on the reporters assigned to those beats. We never quite got beyond the demands of the day-to-day, which meant that although there was a general commitment to in-depth projects there was seldom the time to do them. I did have several reporters more or less at my disposal, but even they had partial responsibility for other day-to-day coverage.

I was also night city editor, but on a P.M. paper there's very little for the night city editor to do. I did my best to keep busy, but found that turf was jealously guarded and my efforts to take on additional responsibilities were generally rebuffed. The purported staff expansion (and concurrent opportunities for upward mobility) didn't materialize. Within months I came to the unhappy conclusion that (1) I didn't have enough to do, (2) there was no general support for giving me anything else to do, and (3) no good prospects the situation would change.

I learned a couple of lessons: Forget what you're told about what may materialize in the future. All you're being hired for is the job that is open. If that doesn't appeal to you, you're wasting your time.

Even if it does appeal to you, take a careful look around. Find out exactly what it is you'll be doing. How many staff members will you supervise? Will they also report to someone else? Does your immediate supervisor know of this arrangement? Does he or she support it? You have lots more bargaining power before you're hired than once you're on board.

I again started sending out resumes. I must have sent out dozens. The cover letter summarized my broad range of experience and explained my objective was to be managing editor. I started flying around the country for interviews—sometimes at their expense, sometimes at my own. Most involved positions not too different from the job I then held.

And then I heard from Champaign, Illinois. They needed an executive editor. It was not the best of situations. The previous executive editor had been fired in a dispute with the publisher. The newsroom (understandably) was upset. The publisher (understandably) was upset. She felt the staff was challenging her authority by taking the side of the person she'd fired.

I found out what I could about the paper and the community. It was the home of the University of Illinois, a relatively sophisticated, nice place to live. The economy was stable. The staff was reported to be young, good, professional. I flew out for an interview, and came away with a generally good feeling. Perhaps it was not the ideal situation, but it was the job I wanted.

Before I say more about why it has turned out so well for me, I think it's important to say something about the places I didn't go and places I didn't even consider. Some news organizations have a bad reputation in how they treat women employees. Some are sexist in hiring. Some will hire but not promote. Most of these are changing, but too slowly for my tastes. Partly because I got into newspaper management somewhat late, I figured I didn't have the time to go places where I'd be held back simply because I was a woman. I didn't have the time to spend proving I was twice as good as a man. I also, quite frankly, had no desire to waste my time playing that game.

I consciously made a decision not to go anyplace where I got bad vibrations about my status as a woman. That usually came up during the interview. I could tell by the questions asked or the responses I got that my interviewer was having problems about my being a woman, especially a married woman. I think one can also get a pretty good sense of how women are treated by looking around the newsroom or reading several recent issues of the *Editor and Publisher Yearbook*. How many women are there in the newsroom? How many in management? How old are they? Newsrooms that have a number of young women on less prestigious beats may be learning. Those that have had women for years handling important assignments and serving as editors generally don't have managers who still need to be convinced that women can do the job.

I've not worked on a single paper where I felt there was a special burden to prove myself because I was a woman. Not all papers are sexist.

I have a small circle of friends I've called every time I've considered a career move. They've worked at various papers around the country and know the specifics and generalities of numerous newspaper operations. I think it's very important to check out the reactions of some neutral, knowledgeable third parties when a job change looms. My friends have advised me against taking certain jobs by pointing out things I hadn't considered. To them I'm grateful.

It wouldn't be quite accurate to say there were no problems being accepted by the staff or the community in Champaign, but the problems didn't relate to my being a woman. There was a certain wait-and-see that simply reflected the fact that my predecessor had been fired. What kind of person would step into that situation? What kind of person would be chosen? That I was a woman was far less important to the staff than what my management style would be. My natural style is low-key, strong on collective decision making. I think it was the right style for this situation. I had inherited several excellent young male editors whose judgment I quickly learned I could trust. I needed to learn about staff personalities and newsroom procedures. They obliged. I had no desire to make changes just for the sake of change or to stamp my "personality" on the product.

Happily, we shared the same goals: putting out a hard-news product heavy on local news, emphasizing and expanding in-depth coverage. I'm sure they had their reservations about me, but I honestly don't think they were particularly concerned about my being female. If anything, they may have tried harder to get along just to prove they didn't object to a woman boss.

Men in their late twenties and early thirties have grown up in a world in which it was assumed women would have careers. Most feel keenly that sexism—like racism—is wrong. Men who object to working for a woman often fall into two categories: They grew up in the "old school" and simply refuse to join the modern world, or they're fundamentally insecure about their own abilities and use sexism as a weapon to increase their standing in the business world. My editors are good. They know it. They know I appreciate how good they are.

Neither my publisher nor my immediate boss, the editor and general manager, had gone looking for a woman. They simply felt I was well qualified for the job and that my educational background was well suited to a university community. Both of them made a special effort not only to support my standing within the newspaper, but also to introduce me early on to influential people in the community. There was a clear public message of confidence in my abilities and the community response was equally positive. Many people, in fact, told me how delighted they were that the paper had hired a woman.

To some extent, that acceptance reflects the fact that Champaign-Urbana is a university community. That I have a Ph.D. was icing on the cake, but I don't think a woman without one would necessarily have had a hard time.

Nevertheless, what counts in management is results. I figured I had about a week to prove myself to the staff and a couple of months to prove myself to the community. Had I been ineffective, unable to handle the job, the negative reaction might have been stronger because I was a woman. From the beginning, my boss, the editor, adopted a hands-off approach. On a day-to-day basis, I'm in charge of the newsroom. He's been very good about leaving the day-to-day operation to me. He was worried at first that I needed to establish a firmer presence, assert my authority more. I sensed, however, that I'd win acceptance and cooperation much sooner with a gentler stance.

I don't come on like gangbusters. That doesn't mean I'm not in charge.

The only aspect of my personal life anyone finds troubling is that my husband lives in California. University communities tend to be more accepting of such arrangements than most, but some people still feel awkward asking whether my husband's in town. I don't think the lack of a live-in spouse hampers my ability to socialize. The invitations come mainly to "Susan Miller." Sometimes they come to "Susan and Allen Miller." Sometimes they come to "Susan and Bud (if he's in town)."

I have no qualms about going to a social gathering alone. One of my best friends here is another professional woman whose husband works near Washington, D.C. We spend a lot of time discussing job-related problems in a general sense, such as communication, evaluations, morale.

I've found it's very important to have people with whom I can discuss management problems. I've always done that with my husband. Sometimes it's enough just to articulate the problem. In hearing yourself describe it, you begin to realize how to solve it. Beyond that, you need someone whose judgment you trust and who knows you well enough to put what you're saying in context. Bud has a keen instinct for management issues. I often wonder how he learned such things. Some of it may have been his upbringing: He grew up expecting to be in charge someday and he paid attention to how other people did it. It took me a lot longer to realize such things were important and to begin to try to figure them out.

I've also developed a circle of friends among other women editors, primarily through membership in American Society of Newspaper Editors and Associated Press Managing Editors. Janet Brandt, managing editor of the *Journal-American* in Bellevue, Washington, and I arranged a breakfast for the women editors who attended the APME convention in San Diego last fall. It was a good way to make contacts and we're going to make it an annual event.

Of the women who currently hold top management positions, every one is someone special. They are friendly, accessible, helpful. Their company is delightful. I have no trouble interacting with the male editors in these organizations, but there's a special kind of shorthand that women editors talk. Or maybe it's just easier to say to another woman: "I've got a problem. What do I do?"

What is my management style? Basically, it's low-key and collective. Some managers are still hung up on the "show them who's boss" approach. Authority shared isn't authority lost. No one person always knows best. Having the guts to share authority is to me the ultimate measure of self-confidence.

I think there's an often overlooked side benefit to collective decision making: It shares the stress. Although some of my editors initially were uncomfortable about my openness and my candor, they have learned to deal with it and to become more open in return. I can discuss anything with them. I have no qualms about saying: "Here's the problem. I don't know what to do. Help me figure it out." They come to me with their problems. We trust each other and we trust each other's advice. It's not only a supportive situation, it's a healthy situation. It takes a lot of the strain out of managing.

Although I think an executive editor has a responsibility to help shape and define the direction of news content, I do not feel I have the right to redesign it or redefine it according to my personal tastes and interests. While an editor may help a community raise its sights by improving the quality and the depth of its newspaper coverage, every community has the right to a newspaper that reflects its interests and concerns, its tastes and standards. I'm disturbed by what I see as a trend towards some editors' redesigning newspapers to reflect either their own interests or whatever is journalistically in vogue, and then imposing these formulas on community after community as they move around the country. There is little interest in whether the perfect formula or the latest trend is appropriate to a given community. I guess I feel that being an editor is a bit like the ministry is supposed to be: It's stewardship, not an ego trip.

Another part of being a good manager is giving people the tools they need to do their jobs. That means everything from dictionaries to written policies that take the guesswork out of accepting a free lunch (we won't). Quality management depends on planning, evaluating, and most especially, hiring and promoting with an absolute eye to quality. I'm as interested in style as results. An employee's attitude is important. I won't abide prima donnas or whiners. And I insist on careful, thorough, grown-up management from all of the editors under me.

Careful hiring is probably the most important thing an executive editor does. I feel strongly that it ought to be a team effort. The person who will supervise the employee has to be convinced the right person has been chosen.

The second most important thing I can do is make sure the right people are in the right management spots in my newsroom. There's a sense of commitment here that continues to amaze me. The people on my staff are, by and large, crazy about their work. That's partially due to the fact that most of my staff are fairly young. It's due even more to the fact that my editors are, for the most part, excellent. Some I inherited. Some I hired. Some I promoted. I have an absolute obligation to my staffers to give them the best editors I can find. If an editor doesn't meet my standards, I'll counsel that person. If that doesn't work, I'll make changes.

The editors in my newsroom now are absolutely solid. I trust their judgment. I trust their discretion. I can walk out of here for a day or a week and know everything is in good hands.

That doesn't mean I take a totally hands-off approach. I insist on lots of planning—not only what's going in this day's paper, but also on planning ahead. That means planning for the Sunday edition, which is our showcase for the best of our in-depth stories. It means planning major story topics a month at a time, sitting down with all of my section editors, hearing their ideas, refining those ideas, and deciding who'll handle what. It means long-range planning every six months: asking editors to assess our progress and needs, set priorities, agree on goals.

All of this planning initially caused some editors to bridle. Planning does take time. But it also pays off—in better utilization of staff, overall productivity, and most of all, quality.

Our commitment to in-depth reporting, to extensive planning, and to quality hiring has paid dividends. Recently the *News-Gazette* took five first-place and three second-place awards in the annual competition of the Illinois Press Association. We were competing against all newspapers of more than 5,000 circulation, and we set a record for the most firsts won by a single newspaper in a single year. Contests aren't everything, but they do mean you're doing something right. And they're nice for staff morale.

I'm aware it's all too easy for a manager to spend most of the time with the marginal performers, the ones who cause problems. I sometimes have to make a conscious effort to pay attention to my solid performers and stars, tell them they're doing a good job, find out what they'd like to do next.

Part of being a good manager is evaluating people—everybody—on a regular basis. People deserve to be told explicitly what their weaknesses are. They need to hear periodically what their strengths are. If I consistently ignore a performance weakness, I let down that person and everyone else in the newsroom.

I also believe strongly in private criticism and public praise. A bulletin board should be for clips and comments (from me or other editors) about jobs well done. People don't deserve public embarrassment when they botch up. They need a prompt, firm, private explanation of what they did wrong. Sometimes they need a written reprimand. Sometimes they need formal probation. But they never, ever deserve to be publicly embarrassed. That is the sure sign of an insensitive and immature manager.

My management style is still evolving. A big part of what I'm working on now is a sense of timing—knowing when to move on something, how hard to push, setting standards that are reasonable, but that give everyone something to reach for.

How would any of this have been different for a man?

I think much of my interest in good management, effective management, stems from being a woman. Most of my understanding of careers and career advancement I've learned from men.

Women of my generation were brought up to put a premium on people's feelings, on getting along, on what, in an office, is morale. I care as much about the process of producing news content as I do about the finished product. I firmly believe there's a high correlation between quality management and a quality product. But I can't prove that, and even if someone demonstrated me wrong, I'd go right on caring about the atmosphere in my newsroom and how my employees treat one another.

Wandering around the country as a graduate student wife didn't do much for my career, but it did put me in a variety of work situations under a variety of management styles. I've been fortunate to have had some excellent managers. I've worked for some very talented people who were mediocre managers. And I've worked for some people who were, as managers, terrible. From those experiences I've distilled much of what I believe about management. I also make it a point to read as many books and articles as I can.

I think that, as a woman, I'm less inclined to toy with the macho "I'm in charge here" style of management. It may be appropriate in some newsrooms. It wouldn't have been appropriate in mine.

I've been fortunate to have a husband, a circle of friends and several bosses who have been extremely supportive of my career. They've helped me figure out a career path. They've taught me what to look out for in a job, how to negotiate, how to plan ahead.

To some extent, I've gotten ahead because I've been willing to take fairly drastic measures. There's no question that getting the Ph.D. was a big boost to my career. It has been a major factor in my being considered for various jobs. To the extent it is true that a woman has to be more qualified than a man, I am. To the extent I lost ground in my career by following my husband around, I made up for it by getting that degree. But even with the Ph.D., I had to start out as a reporter and prove myself.

The other major factor in advancing my career was my willingness to go where the job was and live apart from my husband. One can argue that, as times goes on, there will be more commuter marriages. One can argue that there will be more men committed to their wives' careers.

So far, I hear a lot of pious talk about that in a lot of enlightened circles. So far, there aren't very many husbands like mine. There aren't very many couples who would be willing to live as we do. There aren't very many married executive editors. That tells us something, doesn't it?

Jane Mohnen

MARJORIE PAXSON

Jane Mohnen

MARJORIE PAXSON

Marjorie Paxson

MARJORIE PAXSON, publisher of the *Muskogee Phoenix,* has been in the newspaper business since she was graduated from the University of Missouri School of Journalism in 1944.

Her career experience includes working for the then United Press in Lincoln, Nebraska, 1944-46; the Associated Press in Omaha, 1946-48; the *Houston Post,* 1948-52; the *Houston Chronicle,* 1952-56; the *Miami Herald,* 1956-68; the *St. Petersburg Times,* 1968-70; the *Philadelphia Bulletin,* 1970-76; the *Idaho Statesman,* Boise, 1976-78. She became publisher and editor of the *Public Opinion* in Chambersburg, Pennsylvania, in February 1978 and was transferred to Muskogee on October 6, 1980.

She has twice been associated with special newspapers published during United Nations world conferences. In June 1975, she was editor of the daily tabloid published in Mexico City for the UN International Women's Year conference, and in July 1980, she was associate editor of the daily paper for the UN Mid-Decade for Women conference in Copenhagen.

She is a past national president of Theta Sigma Phi, now Women in Communications, Inc. and was named a national headliner by that group in 1976. She is listed in *Who's Who of American Women.* She was a Penney-Missouri winner in 1970 while she was women's editor of the *St. Petersburg Times.*

My involvement in journalism began in 1939 during my junior year at Lamar High School in Houston when I took a class in journalism and worked on our school paper. By the end of that semester I was hooked. I've never been sorry.

My teacher had gone to the University of Missouri School of Journalism, so that's where I went. After graduation in June 1944, I landed a job with the then United Press in Lincoln, Nebraska. This was during World War II when women were welcomed in newsrooms and by the wire services. My salary was $25 a week.

Our two-woman office was at the top of the stairs in the Journal building. With two desks, a file cabinet and two teletype machines in place, there was barely room for bureau manager Marguerite Davis and me. We were separated from the newspaper's morgue by chicken wire.

Today, as publisher of the *Muskogee,* Oklahoma, *Phoenix,* I work in a

121

beautifully furnished, cherry-paneled office at least five times larger than that tiny cage in Lincoln. A Salvador Dali print, *Joan of Arc,* hangs on one wall; two batiks from India are on another. The blue pillow in one corner belongs to Tiger, my dachshund who comes to work with me. My annual salary is several thousand times larger than my first weekly wage.

The road from Lincoln to Muskogee took many turns—to Omaha, home to Houston, to Miami, across Florida to St. Petersburg, north to Philadelphia, almost across the continent to Boise, Idaho, back east to Chambersburg, Pennsylvania, and finally to Oklahoma. There were side trips to Mexico City, Washington, D.C., and Copenhagen, Denmark.

Obviously I have been willing to move, but then moving was easier for me because I never married. Sometimes along the way I got equal pay. That was true when I worked for the wire services in Nebraska and it's true now. In between was another matter.

I've been lucky. For example, when I was laid off by UP in 1946, the Associated Press offered me a job in Omaha—at more money.

Like most women during World War II, when I took the UP reporting job, I signed a waiver that I would relinquish the job to a man when the soldiers came back from the war. None of us thought anything about it; signing that waiver was standard procedure.

The UP fired a good many women in the fall of '46, including me. However, this may be one of the few times on record that a woman was replaced by a man at a lower salary. I was at the second-year grade under the Guild contract and he was hired at the beginning level.

My luck was running right in 1975 when I was named editor of an eight-page daily tabloid published in Mexico City during the United Nations World Conference for International Women's Year. Editing that newspaper was the hardest work I have ever done and also is probably the single most important thing I have accomplished.

The lucky part is how I got the job. The Non-Governmental Organizations affiliated with the UN were holding a parallel meeting to the World Conference and, as usual, they would put out a daily paper. The NGO leadership wanted a qualified woman editor who could direct straight down-the-middle coverage of the events.

A volunteer in their New York City office was asked to find the editor. "Call around the country. Get leads," were her instructions. This volunteer was originally from Philadelphia and had attended Temple University. She had not majored in journalism but she had taken a journalism course at Temple. So she called her former journalism teacher and he suggested me.

On the afternoon of Monday, April 28, she called. It didn't take long for me to accept and by the next afternoon I had a leave of absence to spend five weeks during June and early July in Mexico City.

Top newsroom management at the *Philadelphia Bulletin,* where I was an assistant metro editor, allowed me to take the time to go to Mexico but they weren't very happy about it. The *Bulletin* did not print anything about my Mexico City assignment and would not run the four-part series I wrote about the IWY meetings when I returned. (I did sell the series to some other papers around the country.)

I decided it was time to get out. But I was fifty-two and friends were saying that newspapering was for the young and that I would have to switch careers and go into public relations or some other journalism-related field.

On November 1, 1975, I wrote to Al Neuharth, president of the Gannett Company, Inc. in Rochester, New York. He had given me good advice sixteen years earlier at the *Miami Herald* and I figured he would give me a straight answer now.

Al and I went to work for the *Herald* around the same time in 1956—he in the city room and I on the copy desk in the women's department. He moved up to assistant managing editor and I was promoted to assistant women's editor. In the fall of 1959, I unexpectedly was offered the women's editor slot on one of the Atlanta papers. I was stunned. I wasn't job-hunting; I had been promoted in May, loved my work and the *Herald* had sent me to an API seminar on women's pages in New York City in June. I certainly did not want to move, and yet. . . .

On the suggestion of *Herald* Women's Editor Marie Anderson, I talked with Al. He straightened out my thinking in a hurry. The gist of his advice was this:

You've got to decide for yourself and you can't let loyalty stand in the way. It's your career. Forget that you've just been promoted and that the *Herald* sent you to API. Go up there and find out for yourself what the job is all about. Then make up your mind.

"Remember," and these were his exact words, "nobody is going to look out for Marj Paxson except Marj Paxson."

So years later, I asked Al for his appraisal on "whether someone my age can even make a good move" in the newspaper business. Al's reply was scribbled across the bottom of my letter: "Call me collect in Rochester." I did and his comment was, "That's the silliest question I've ever heard."

The upshot was a job interview at Gannett headquarters in Rochester, and thereby hangs another tale of luck.

The interview was set for a Monday, my day off. I had reservations on the one direct flight from Philadelphia to Rochester. But on Sunday, the airline went on strike. Any other connnections were impossible. Change in Pittsburgh, or change in Buffalo, or change somewhere else and spend hours en route.

I had learned from one disastrous job interview when I flew all night and was too tired to make sense that one does not go into such a meeting exhausted. I called my Gannett contact in Rochester Sunday afternoon and said I couldn't get there from here.

Within hours she called back. "If you can be at the North Philadelphia airport at 8 A.M.," she said, "the company jet will pick you up."

They didn't send the jet just for me, of course. The board of directors was meeting that Monday in Rochester and the jet picked up me, and director Bill Stretch, from Camden, New Jersey, and then went on to Washington, D.C., for directors William P. Rogers, the former secretary of state, and Jack Webb, who had headed NASA. The same jet returned me home that evening.

The next day my Gannett contact called again. "Okay, we've talked with you," she said. "Now you have to tell us. What are your goals? What do you want to do? What do you want to be? Write me a letter."

Before I could look forward, I had to look back. Mexico City was just behind me. My title was editor, but I had hired the staff, directed the coverage in both English and Spanish, supervised the page make-up, made the arrangements for printing. Actually I had been the publisher.

From 1963 to 1967 I had been national president of Theta Sigma Phi, now called Women In Communications, Inc. During that time I had turned the organization from a narrow, journalistic social sorority concept to a professional approach. I had motivated volunteers who paid dues for the privilege of working in the organization to want to change direction.

Over the years, I had run women's departments on four newspapers.

My reply listed three options: managing editor, editor of an editorial page or publisher.

Gannett came through in the summer of 1976 and I went to Boise as assistant managing editor of the *Idaho Statesman*. Eighteen months later I became a publisher on two days' notice and moved once more, this time to Chambersburg, Pennsylvania, as editor and publisher of the *Public Opinion*. That lasted until October 6, 1980, when I became publisher in Muskogee.

Stepping into a new situation is never easy. Everybody knows you're the boss, naturally, but it's important to do some special thing to establish yourself.

In Chambersburg, the walls of the advertising department and the business office were a horrid orange. I had them repainted off-white.

On the way in from the Muskogee airport, the former owner and retiring publisher of the *Phoenix* said, "You might as well know before you hear it at the paper that I have had a firm policy that women cannot wear pantsuits to work."

I had come prepared to look every inch the lady publisher—heels, hose, tailored suits, the whole bit. But I changed gears. Next morning I walked into the building wearing the only pantsuit I had brought with me, and at my first department head meeting, I announced a policy change. Some women in the plant went out that evening to buy pantsuits for work the next day.

My career has not always been onward and upward. There have been lateral moves, periods of stagnation, and times of total frustration.

I still have not quite forgiven women's movement activists for turning against women's editors. In the early days of the movement in the sixties, most substantive newspaper coverage of the movement was on the women's pages. I considered myself a part of the movement and so did many other women's editors I knew across the country.

But the activists wanted the movement news off our pages and in their eyes, we women's editors were traitors.

When editors responded by changing women's sections to general interest feature sections, women's editors paid the price. We were not considered capable of directing this new kind of feature section. That was man's work.

I shuddered every time I read another story in *Editor & Publisher* about a paper making the switch and the former women's editor either being demoted or given the lateral two-step.

I know how they felt because it happened to me—not once, but twice.

On the *St. Pete Times,* the change was made the Tuesday after Labor Day, 1969, and I ended up as the No. 3 person in the new setup. In December the *Times* was notified that I had won a Penney-Missouri award for general excellence of the now-defunct women's pages. In May 1970, six weeks after I went to Columbia, Missouri, to accept that award, I was fired.

I landed on my feet as women's editor of the *Philadelphia Bulletin.* But . . . in 1973, again on the Tuesday after Labor Day, the *Bulletin* abolished its women's section for a Focus section with a male editor and I was exiled to the Sunday magazine as associate editor.

The next fourteen months were the blackest of my life. On the magazine, I read proof and handled petty details. Incoming manuscripts were given to other staffers for evaluation and I was never involved in the planning or with photos and layout.

I hated it. But there was a recession on, new jobs were hard to find and at least I did have a regular paycheck. I worked off my frustration by pulling weeds in the yard and by depending on friends for support.

My lowest point came at a women's meeting where I felt free to talk about what had happened to me. One of the participants heard me out and then told me:

"Marj, you have to accept the fact that you're a casualty of the women's movement."

There was one ray of hope. In the reshuffle when I went to the Sunday magazine, I was given the additional title of editor of women's news. My responsibility in that capacity was to attend the daily news meeting and to point out news of special interest to women.

I was determined to attend those news meetings, to participate and to stay visible. Eventually, in the fall of 1974, I became assistant metro editor in charge of the eighteen beat reporters.

The long night was over. Now I had to regain my self-confidence. For some time on the metro desk, even after I'd been to an API seminar for city editors, I was super cautious. Every detail of an assignment was cleared with metro editor Jim Tunnell. One day he had enough.

"You're wasting time," he said. "You act like somebody who's been badly burned. Go ahead and do it. I trust your judgment."

Mexico City finished what Jim started. Finally I was back in full stride.

Between Philadelphia and Boise, I spent three months as a consultant to the United States International Women's Year Commission. There I helped with the production of the Commission's report to the President, ". . . To Form a More Perfect Union . . . Justice for American Women."

When the United Nations held its Mid-Decade for Women International Conference in Copenhagen in July 1980, the NGOs called me again about the daily paper. This time, however, with anti-American sentiment running so high in the UN, there was no way I could have the top spot. I was happy to have my hand in as an assistant editor.

Moving is always rough and the hardest part, I think, is getting settled in a new home. I never really feel relaxed until I have pictures on the wall. But unpacking and all that takes time just when I'm trying to learn a new job and how to work with a whole new staff. These are the times I call in my "support system"—my brother and sister-in-law.

John and Peggy pitched in when I moved from Florida to Philadelphia. He is a professor at Edinboro State College in northwest Pennsylvania, so they drove down for a week. Peggy does whatever needs doing. I came home one afternoon to find her washing windows. John and I had great arguments on how high to hang the pictures because he's six inches taller than I. But I couldn't have done it so quickly without them.

Peggy was also on hand for the moves from Boise to Chambersburg and from there to Muskogee, thanks to Gannett. The company will pay for the visit of a spouse to the new location. "Since I don't have a spouse," I asked the corporate personnel officer, "will you pay for my sister-in-law to come and help me move?"

After a pause, the answer was, "Yes, we can do that."

Once the unpacking is over and I'm becoming accustomed to my new job, it's time to establish myself in the community. I make speeches at every invitation. Being a native Texan helps. My string of Texas jokes is almost endless and there's one to fit just about every occasion.

I also have a one-liner which I use every time I speak to a male audience. Invariably the man introducing me will ask whether I want to be called "Miss, or M-z-z-z?"

"Don't call me Miss, call me Ms.," I answer, "because I haven't missed as much as you think I have."

During my four years as national president of Theta Sigma Phi, I acquired a collection of big, flashy costume jewelry rings. The theory was that if the delegates to the national convention got bored with my presiding, they could always focus on my hands. I still wear a big ring whenever I speak.

Those four years were busy, sometimes even hectic. My expense receipts showed that I visited forty chapters and clubs, traveling more than 75,000 miles, mostly on weekends. I made so many speeches that I got over being nervous in front of a microphone.

I learned a lot about time management and about how to organize my thoughts and set priorities. My best guess—again from expense receipts—is that I wrote more than 4,000 letters, an average of twenty-five a week for 208 weeks. Some were done at the office but most were done at home before going to work.

My early morning routine ran like this: Up promptly at 6 A.M. Plug in the coffee pot, turn on the oven and set the timer for 6:20. Write letters. At the sound of the timer, pour a cup of coffee and put a TV dinner in the oven. (Frozen breakfasts had not yet come along.) Reset the timer for 6:50. Write more letters. At the sound of the timer, remove the TV dinner from the oven. While it cooled slightly, gather up everything to be mailed. Pour another cup of coffee. Eat breakfast. Skim the morning paper. Dress and go to work.

Gradually, through all my experience, I have evolved the approach that I do what I need to do in the way most comfortable for me. I try to speak up and simply be myself. Above all, I do not want to be like a man.

My management style involves a lot of persuasion and teaching, a little preaching and occasionally behaving like a Double S-O-B (that's "boss" spelled backward). I want to get everyone involved in a team effort, taking a positive approach to whatever problem we're dealing with. I keep pushing and prodding, asking questions and more questions.

I try to be quick with criticism and just as quick with praise. I can be very patient, especially on big things. It's the little things that trigger my temper.

My bosses along the way have had a lot to do with how my management style developed. Happily, I can report that some of the best bosses I've had have been women. Some of the men were helpful and some were not.

In Lincoln, Maggie Davis taught me that even though I was a graduate of the famous Missouri J-School, I didn't know everything there was to know about journalism. I still don't.

Oveta Culp Hobby of the *Houston Post* taught me the importance of backing up your staff and not giving in to outside pressure.

Back in the late forties or early fifties while I was at the *Houston Post,* the decision was made to take brides off the front page of the Society section. As women's editor, I had to tell parents that their daughters' wedding portraits would not be on our Sunday section page. One father went over my head to the publisher's office and Mrs. Hobby. She personally notified me that the new policy should be followed.

I have thought of her often since becoming a publisher and facing the same kinds of pressures.

Dorothy Jurney, who hired me at the *Miami Herald,* taught me how to deal with people, how to be fair and honest and tough and how to demand the best—and get it. Her use of the sandwich technique—a compliment, the criticism and another closing compliment—was superb.

Marie Anderson, who succeeded Dorothy at the *Herald,* taught me how to set high standards and how to quietly, patiently stick to your guns to maintain them. Marie won the Penney-Missouri top award so many years in a row they once threw her out for twelve months.

Because these women helped me, I believe in taking every opportunity to help young people. If I've got it made, I should help the rest of them as they come along.

My advice to young women—and men—is to be a specialist and to learn everything they can about their own jobs. Then, begin to be a generalist and learn something about every job that touches theirs. Moving up in a career means seeing the broader picture and understanding how other departments work.

Advancing in a career can bring problems, can require personal sacrifices and frequently can mean loneliness. That's all part of the climb. There have been times when I moved to a new town that I've found I did not talk to anyone but a salesperson all weekend.

When I finished J-School, my dream was to become a foreign correspondent. After four years with UP and AP, I realized that was nonsense. So I decided that becoming editor of a major women's page would be my ultimate goal.

I reached that point but it didn't last. When Gannett offered me the opportunity, I set new sights. Deep down inside, I guess I have always been a "closet boss." Now I have come out of the closet.

My job as publisher is the best job I have ever had. It's almost like being the conductor of an orchestra. When everyone is in tune, playing at the same tempo with the same feeling, you can make beautiful music. Yes, being a publisher carries more risk, more responsibilities and more headaches. But it also is more fun.

What more can anyone ask?

Meriden City Manager Dana Miller, right, with Barbara C. White and Carter H. White. At left is Audrea Miller.

Barbara C. White

BARBARA C. WHITE is editor of the *Meriden,* Connecticut, *Record-Journal,* a 30,000-circulation morning newspaper. She describes herself as "one of a disappearing breed—a member of a Mom and Pop team which runs a family-owned newspaper." Her husband, Carter White, is publisher of the newspaper. Mrs. White graduated from Radcliffe with high honors and a Phi Beta Kappa key in 1939. At Radcliffe, she worked as a correspondent for the *Boston Herald.* After graduation, she worked for a company newspaper for a year before she married Carter White in 1940.

I am one of a disappearing breed—a member of a Mom and Pop team which runs a family-owned newspaper. My husband's parents managed the paper in the same way, he as publisher and owner, she as editor and editorial policymaker. It was a wonderfully fruitful arrangement.

Before them, the editor and half-owner shared his writing and thinking responsibilities with an associate editor, whom he eventually married.

My own involvement in journalism began while I was a student at Radcliffe and correspondent for the *Boston Herald.* I received a degree with high honors and a Phi Beta Kappa key in 1939. My publisher and spouse, Carter H. White, received a degree in English literature also from Harvard College in 1938 and went on to graduate from Harvard Law School in 1941. I worked for a company newspaper for a year before we married in 1940.

It took about fifteen years to struggle through the war and get three children on their feet so I could return to full-time newspapering which had been my intent, with family concurrence. During those years I worked mostly at home, writing editorials through frequent phone consultations, attendance at public meetings, and participation in city affairs to get firsthand knowledge of the area. My husband had similar involvement: He served as a state senator and as the city's corporation counsel among his other duties before he gave up the practice of law for full-time newspaper work.

I learned the newsroom side of the business on the smaller of our two papers, the afternoon *Journal,* where I served as editorial page editor and as a general fill-in on both papers at the society desk, and dummying and filling inside pages generally. I also wrote columns on a variety of subjects—principally reviewing plays, but also books, movies, restaurants and writing features, both cityside and society. My principal responsibility, and the one I took most seriously, was editorial writing.

About ten years ago, a decision was made to phase out the *Journal* and combine it with the *Record* as a morning paper. I served as editor of the *Journal* in these years, after the retirement of its long-time editor, and participated in the plans for combination. After the *Record-Journal* was established, I served as associate editor and executive editor and at the retirement of the *Record's* editor, I was named to replace him.

Much is said about the electronic revolution, but the revolution of how print gets on paper has been much closer to me and, because I understand it more thoroughly, much more fascinating. I began at the end of the old hot type days; one of my first contacts with it was working a Kellogg keyboard affixed to a Linotype machine during a strike. Later I learned to read hot lead lines backward and upside down and the inflexible limits that exist on a printed page.

The first afternoon of cold type, when I raced up the stairs to what we then called the composing room and heard no klacking and banging, I wanted to shout, "Hey, get busy or we won't have a paper." It took us a long time to get over the habit of stopping by the plant on Sunday morning to see that the gas was lit under the lead pots, ready for operation that night.

Our first computer was a baby model that took the product of our taped material and justified the line lengths. We had bought it from a couple of young MIT scientists and when it became obsolete, as it did all too soon, they begged it back and put it to work on a project that was keeping track of the world's whale population. It may still be operating.

Every two or three years the process changed. We learned to type on IBM Selectrics and to proofread our own efforts. The composing room became the Graphics Department, the few remaining printers took off their aprons and put on neckties, and editors suddenly found themselves responsible for their own mistakes. What you write is what you get.

Our switch to video terminals in 1981 was the most traumatic for all of us. I went at it eagerly delighted with the idea of being in complete control of my product, but I found that the mechanical work of correcting, proofreading and layout has taken an enormous slice of my creative energies.

We have met the challenge by adding highly skilled people to the copy desk and all the staff except a few old-timers (me among them, but secretly) find this is the most natural of all ways to operate.

Obviously, in an ownership position and with strong management backing, I have had minimal difficulties because of my gender. I have found that a thorough knowledge of what I'm doing is especially important if I am to be taken seriously by the staff and the public. I have also affirmed the need to assert myself beyond the natural inclination of women of my generation, especially with other editors. I find myself always standing to talk to people who stand in front of me, wearing tailored clothes, shaping my accent to communicate more clearly with various kinds of people.

I have watched newsroom attitudes toward women change, but slowly.

The sexism isn't as obvious but it's there. We have had many brilliant women in the newsroom and we brag about them—the only female city editor in Connecticut for a while, an outstanding woman wire editor, the sharpest police reporter ever we had. One of our copy editors is a woman, and we just lost a brilliant political reporter to another paper.

But the staff is still not balanced. One editor of a suburban bureau insists on even numbers—two of each—and holds out till he gets them. But too often the city room with its fifteen or so newspeople has only two or three women above the clerk-typist level. Most don't stay with us long enough to qualify for higher positions; the best are in big demand at larger papers.

We encourage women to carry on through pregnancies and to stay with us afterwards, making as many accommodations as possible well beyond the three-months postpartum level, but few can stick with a full-time job. At this level, our best luck is with women who have come back to us through part-time and later full-time work over several years, or those who start part time with small children and work into full-time positions.

NANCY WOODHULL

NANCY WOODHULL

Nancy Woodhull

NANCY WOODHULL, 37, has been a *USA TODAY* planning editor
since January 1982.

Previously she was managing editor of the *Rochester Democrat and
Chronicle*. She joined the *Rochester Times-Union* in 1975 after working at
the *Detroit Free Press* where she progressed from night city editor to
assistant managing editor. She then became managing editor of the
Times-Union and subsequently managing editor of the *Democrat and
Chronicle* in May 1980.

A native of New Jersey, she is a member of the American Society of
Newspaper Editors.

There must be many who think of a managing editor in terms of Lou
Grant's Charlie Hume. Well, I still have a newspaper.

Seriously, every managing editor at every metropolitan newspaper has
not just one—but probably several Lou Grants to help manage the
reporting and editing staff. The managing editor and his or her Lou
Grants get together several times a day to figure out what you will want to
read about in the next day's newspaper. While we're deciding what to do,
there are people in the newsroom doing the work.

I started out as a proofreader in New Jersey and worked my way from
reporter to features editor at a small daily. Then it was on to a short stint
as an art gallery owner. At twenty-eight I was reporting for a larger
metropolitan paper in Detroit. Then seven years ago it was Rochester; a
year ago, Washington.

Though I worked only for three companies in that time, I think every
year I had a different position. It wasn't always a promotion. Just a
different set of responsibilities.

How did I get to be managing editor at *USA TODAY?* Well, I'd like to
think I'm a risk-taker. Not a smart, cagey risk-taker, mind you. Just
someone who was brought up to explore, to try new things, who, as an
adult, was too dumb to say no—maybe when others would have.

I think I became an explorer, thanks to my parents, who though we
didn't have much money, always took my sister and me for Sunday rides.
My father always turned down roads he had never been on before. We'd

135

always get lost, but we'd always get home. Nothing bad ever happened to us.

I really believe the Sunday rides were the beginning of my learning not to play by the rules—at least not by someone else's rules.

The first rule I broke was not finishing college. I only lasted one full year. I disliked college. My span of attention was too short—or maybe the classes were too boring. But I do know that I always felt I couldn't use the information I was learning. I couldn't figure out how I could put it to use at that moment. I am one of those people who must learn by doing, by experiencing things firsthand.

After that one year of college, I applied for the proofreader position at a local newspaper and I got it. A proofreader was the equivalent of being a clerk who compared a reporter's story against what was set in type to check for typographical errors. I thought it was the most exciting job anyone could have and it was my foot in the door of the newspaper business nineteen years ago.

Some people say that things like that don't happen that way anymore. That you can't in this day and age get somewhere without an education, without job contacts, without a specialty. I beg to differ. I see people do it all the time. They bring to their jobs a basic intelligence and enthusiasm.

One of the *Rochester Times-Union's* best writers was a Kelly Girl who signed on for a temporary stint as a clerk a few summers ago. She was the most efficient person I have ever met. She always had time left over to ask if she could do a little reporting. She was willing to do any story. She wasn't looking to be a Woodward or a Bernstein, she just wanted to write. She proved so invaluable we finagled a way to hire her permanently as a clerk. As soon as she was on board, we quickly promoted her to reporter.

There are others like her. Now I have a news assistant who works for me in Washington who didn't finish college and has spent most of his last few years playing in a rock band. But he wants to be a reporter and he has a natural talent for asking questions. And he brings such energy and enthusiasm and willingness to learn to his job that I guarantee that if he keeps that attitude, he can be one of the country's best journalists.

I believe in any stage of our careers, whether we're starting out or trying for the next step up, we can accomplish what we want if we just try—and try with enthusiasm. I don't believe in those books that outline a very structured career path. I guess I don't believe in those career paths because I see them as so inflexible, having so many rules. And I don't know how to play by those rules. I think you find a field you think is very, very interesting and you get any job in it you can, and you do as well as you can, and you just keep asking for more work to do, more responsibilities.

When I was a proofreader I spent every spare moment, after the proofreading was done, of course, writing obituaries and doing rewrites of club news. No one else wanted to do these things. It was considered the drudge work, but I loved it. The editor was so delighted that he found someone who liked to do what everyone else complained about and snubbed their noses at that he hired someone else to do the proofreading and let me do this type of writing full time.

Within about a few months, the editor was moaning about how horrible the education pages—the pages that carried the school news—were. They were also considered the drudge work. I thought it sounded like fun. I thought I could make them better so I volunteered to do the education pages. And, yes, you got it. Again, the editor was so elated that he found someone to get a job done that no one else wanted to do. For a while, I unknowingly made a career doing jobs no one else wanted. The learning by doing these jobs, the learning that I didn't get when I was in college, was my education. It taught me the basics of my business. And the willingness to take on tasks, I believe, got me branded as someone who could get any job done.

Bob Giles, editor of the Gannett Rochester newspaper, says that's why he named me managing editor of the *Times-Union*. And then the managing editor of the *Democrat and Chronicle*. And now I am in Washington at *USA TODAY*, the Nation's Newspaper. And I guess that's success.

I honestly could pinch myself because I'm so excited that things have worked out so well for me. And I'm honored that people think it's so special. But I'm a bit superstitious. It's kind of difficult for me to say I'm successful. Even after surviving nineteen years in the business, even after receiving my fair share of awards and notes of praise from my bosses, and becoming one of the highest ranking women in the business, I still have the feeling that it's all a fantasy, that this can't be happening to me. That someday I'm going to be found out. I guess I run a little scared, always afraid I can't accomplish the next challenge, but I guess I'm a little bit too gutsy not to try.

I am telling you all of this—admitting that I run a little scared—because I don't believe enough people admit that. So often women and men who are successful seem so cool, calm and collected. They seem just like the how-to-dress-and-act-for-success books. And those books make us feel so inadequate. And they make us feel so inadequate because they do not deal with reality. Getting ahead in the everyday world isn't as easy as the books make it sound. It's fun and it's worth it but it isn't without its ups and downs. There have been many days when I didn't want to go to work to face the job—and possibly find out I couldn't do it. But I have learned how to survive and I have learned sometimes it has to hurt for a little while before things work well.

Lucky for me I also have a very close family and very close and loyal friends. I think the books call it a strong support system. My boss in Rochester, Bob Giles, was a very positive motivator. When he asks his employees to do something, he does it in a way that makes you feel that you are the only one capable of doing the job. And if you don't do the job as well as he expects, he doesn't rant and rave. He acts as if he's disappointed because he believes you were capable of so much more.

This kind of working environment was perfect for me to learn in. I was lucky. Some bosses are not so motivating. But even with such a good boss there are some things you don't want to share with them. And that is where networking has proved so valuable to me.

I never imagined myself a member of a network. I always thought being a member of a network was hokey, an unnecessary organizational activity—the equivalent of tea parties for working ladies. That is, I felt that way before I became a member of one. And that was quite by accident.

I was one of about a dozen women interviewed for the basis of an RIT course on women in management. The final night of the course, students and women who were interviewed got together for dinner. Afterwards, a group of women lingered to chat for a while. We took turns describing who we were, why we worked, whether we had children, why we had the aspirations we had. It was so enjoyable, about ten of us decided to meet once a month for a brown bag lunch or brown bag dinner—whatever our busy schedules allowed. That was more than three years ago. That group still meets once a month. They still take turns talking and at each meeting they learn about each other's hopes and dreams and successes and problems. It took just a few meetings before they were asking each other for advice, sharing experiences, helping each other.

I think that had a great bearing on what I did in my job in Rochester the last few years. I had a group of peers whom I trusted, with whom I could share my experiences. But another factor in my success was the Gannett Company.

When I was interviewed for an editor's job at the *Times-Union* seven years ago, a friend there told me that if I worked hard I would have a bright future with Gannett. This pitch was quite different from the one I was hearing from my employer at the *Detroit Free Press.*

First of all, the *Free Press* wasn't quite sure I was editor material. Even though I had been an editor in New Jersey before ever joining the *Free Press* as a reporter. The *Free Press* seemed to say if I would insist, they would give me a try at being an editor. Obviously, Gannett thought I had potential, that I had something to offer. But the *Free Press* would have preferred I stifle my potential. So I went to Rochester and worked my bippy off and I was rewarded with challenging jobs.

There are many people like me in Gannett, people who have gotten where they are because they work hard. Gannett doesn't seem to care whether you're female or you're black or a white male who wears white socks and double knits.

At *USA TODAY* there are almost as many women as men, not only on the general work force but in key management roles. Three of the six managing editors are women. In the newsroom alone, four of the seven key editors are women. And we come from all walks of life and places. My news staff has lived in almost all of the fifty states. And we don't all look alike either. And we don't look like anyone has ever given us a manual on how to dress in Washington. All the company cares about is that we get our work done and done well. With that comes reward.

Seventy-three percent of all 1980 management promotions in Gannett came from within Gannett. The Gannett philosophy has given a lot of people, especially women, a lot of opportunities they might not have had elsewhere. And it has a lot of talented people in high places that other companies might not have thought had the time or inclination for a career commitment.

For instance, Anne Saul, my news editor at *USA TODAY,* is thirty-eight years old and has raised a thirteen-year-old son by herself while progressing from reporter to managing editor of one of Gannett's Florida newspapers and now *USA TODAY.* Janet Sanford, who is the mother of four children, took the risk of quitting her job as associate director of the American Press Institute for a job change at fifty-two years of age to join *USA TODAY* this summer. And Gannett welcomed her with open arms. She is in charge of twelve editors and more than fifty correspondents who compile the state-by-state report that appears each day in *USA TODAY.*

Thirty-seven-year-old Nancy Monaghan, from the *Democrat and Chronicle,* is the day national editor at *USA TODAY.* Nancy once wore a pillbox and white gloves while she trained to be a legal secretary at

Katherine Gibbs School. When she found out that she was as smart as some of the lawyers she worked for, she applied for a job at the *Democrat and Chronicle*. Gannett was wise enough to give her a chance. Her first three days on a tryout, she got three exclusive page-one stories. She was hired, of course, and she hasn't stopped succeeding with Gannett since.

I would say that there are a lot of scrappers like these women on the *USA TODAY* team. A lot of people who have pulled themselves up by the bootstraps. In Gannett, there are sixty-eight publishers among the eighty-eight newspapers in the chain: ten of them are women. That works out to be 14.7 percent as compared to only two percent nationwide in newspapers. The Gannett Company also has two minorities, including a minority female, on its board. And it has a female in the office of the chief executive, and I don't mean a secretary. I mean Madelyn Jennings who is one of four senior vice-presidents. Fifteen and a half percent of Gannett's professionals are minorities, 35.5 percent are female. If Gannett tallied up the percentages of women, minorities, Viet vets, handicapped people, people over forty, etc.—in other words, the people who could be viewed as discriminated classes—we would quickly see that together they represent an overwhelming majority of both our employees and our readers. This means affirmative action is not just a "nice thing to do," it's good business and part of every manager's job—and top managers' bonuses at Gannett are calculated on how well they do in regard to equal employment opportunity.

I also believe that this mix of different sexes and races—of people from different places—is what makes the readers like us at *USA TODAY*. We don't have an East Coast bias. There are too many of us with our roots and pride in the Midwest, the Southwest, and nonmetropolitan areas.

There are too many of us who started as proofreaders. Are we "successful?" We're not done yet.

The late John Dougherty, who was managing editor of the *Times-Union*, always said, "When you are satisfied, tell me, because you need a new job."

New Guardians of the Press

Women at the top of newsroom management face challenges and responsibilities seldom equaled elsewhere in the working world. Whether she's editor of the 13,000-circulation *Herald-Banner* in Greenville, Texas, like Ann Faragher, or planning editor of the 650,000-circulation *USA TODAY* like Nancy Woodhull, she must be many things to many people in many and varied situations. In the corporate hierarchy, she must fit gracefully into the pyramid, acquiring the most admired corporate skills and judiciously playing corporate politics. In the newsroom, she must be a manager as well as a journalist; her skills at motivating creative and educated people must be equally as good as her ability to make judgment calls on the relative news value of that day's offerings. Then, in her community, she must perform on another level altogether: She has obligations to her readers and must establish a relationship with people at all levels of her community. Her professional community demands certain commitments, too, and they are involvements that can be crucial to her professional maturity. Add to that a personal dimension and the attendant choices. And what you have is not a neatly drawn picture of a successful woman editor, but a montage. The stories of the women editors told here are the stories of individuals sharing their experiences: what worked, what didn't, why and how. In sum, they tell you there is no one way to success, no one pattern for a perfect fit. In the end, that may be the happiest news of all.